PERSONAL EFFECTS

A Tale of the Dispossessed

Douglas Post

BROADWAY PLAY PUBLISHING INC
224 E 62nd St, NY, NY 10065
www.broadwayplaypub.com
info@broadwayplaypub.com

PERSONAL EFFECTS
© Copyright 2017 Douglas Post

Cover photography by Roy Hurt and Getty Images, cover design by Don McLean

First edition: October 2017
I S B N: 978-0-88145-736-0

Book design: Marie Donovan
Page make-up: Adobe InDesign
Typeface: Palatino

PERSONAL EFFECTS was developed in part through the Carnegie Mellon Drama Showcase of New Plays in Pittsburgh, Pennsylvania and the Toledo Repertoire Theatre in Toledo, Ohio.

PERSONAL EFFECTS was first produced at the Circle Theatre in Forest Park, Illinois on January 10, 2003. The cast was as follows:

NICHOLAS BARNES	Dan Holahan
RACHEL BARNES	Jen Albert
THE DERELICT	Lester Keefe
MARTIN FLEMING	David Hoke
LOUISE EBRIGHT	Jackie Sidle
HARRISON SEITZ	Jim Schmid
AMELIA BARNES	Catherine Ferraro
SAMUEL GEDDES	Leonard Kraft
JACQUELINE BARNES	Mary O'Dowd
Director	Ty Perry
Set design	Jon Fraizer
Costume design	Ty Perry
Lighting design	Neil Anderson
Sound design	Douglas Post
Production stage manager	Donna Oswald

PERSONAL EFFECTS was the winner of the 1995 Midwestern Playwrights Festival Award.

CHARACTERS & SETTING

NICHOLAS BARNES, *a tax attorney, early 30s*
RACHEL BARNES, *a commercial artist, late 20s*
THE DERELICT, *a transient, mid 20s*
MARTIN FLEMING, NICHOLAS'*s friend, early 30s*
LOUISE EBRIGHT, NICHOLAS'*s lover, mid 20s*
HARRISON SEITZ, *a C E O, early 60s*
AMELIA BARNES, *a farm girl, 19*
SAMUEL GEDDES, *the owner of a parts store, early 80s*
JACQUELINE BARNES, NICHOLAS'*s aunt, late 50s*

Time: A winter night in 1999, then moving back a few months, then moving forward in time to that same night.

Place: The attic of a farmhouse in Evansville, Pennsylvania.

This play is dedicated to Ty Perry and the first company of PERSONAL EFFECTS

"When we forget the past, the past returns."
Bertolt Brecht

ACT ONE

Scene 1

(The attic of a farmhouse in Evansville, Pennsylvania. Or rather the suggestion of an attic. An open space with a vaulted ceiling, a single door, and one large window. The room is sparsely furnished with a few select pieces from another time. Two or three small tables, some antique chairs, a lamp that doesn't work, a pile of old books, an assortment of bottles, boxes and scattered papers. A wooden chest that sits in the corner. An old mattress that is ripped and ruined. Dark spaces and shafts of light. Now there is a flash of lightning followed by the sound of thunder. NICHOLAS is revealed standing at the open window looking out into the darkness. He wears a weather-beaten overcoat, a torn sweater, shirt, pants, and a pair of faded shoes. All of his clothes are wearing thin. And he is drenched. It is night. RACHEL stands at the door observing him. He turns. Sees her. A moment)

NICHOLAS: Didn't hear you come in.

RACHEL: I called from downstairs.

NICHOLAS: Didn't hear.

RACHEL: How...how long have you been...God, Nicholas, you look terrible.

NICHOLAS: Yeah, I know.

RACHEL: You're soaked.

NICHOLAS: I walked from the bus stop in town.

RACHEL: You should have called.

NICHOLAS: No money in the pockets. *(Pause)* I take it you got a job.

RACHEL: Yeah.

NICHOLAS: Where?

RACHEL: For the newspaper. *The County Chronicle.*

NICHOLAS: Doing what?

RACHEL: Layout. I was lucky. They needed someone to start immediately.

NICHOLAS: That's good. *(Pause)* Do you want me to go?

RACHEL: No.

NICHOLAS: Because you don't exactly seem heartened by my presence.

RACHEL: I'm in shock, okay?

NICHOLAS: Okay.

RACHEL: I drove up and saw the light on in the attic. A silhouette. In the window. I thought that they'd reconstructed the plan. That they'd come here. To Evansville. Looking for me.

NICHOLAS: No. It's all over. Finished.

RACHEL: What…happened?

NICHOLAS: You didn't get my letter?

RACHEL: No.

NICHOLAS: That's right. They intercepted the letter. Took it away. Well. Anyway. *(He reaches into the pocket of his overcoat and pulls out a plastic bag.)* Here.

(NICHOLAS holds it out for RACHEL, but she doesn't take it.)

RACHEL: What is it?

NICHOLAS: Some notes I started jotting down. A journal. Of sorts. Everything that's taken place. *(He tosses it onto a table.)* It's there. *(Pause)* Listen, I feel like hell. Can I...clean up or something?

RACHEL: Sure.

NICHOLAS: Water works?

RACHEL: Everything works. The plumbing. Electricity. All of it. The house is mine. Ours, I guess. I mean, if that's what you want.

(NICHOLAS and RACHEL stand looking at each other. She breaks the moment and goes to the table. She looks at the journal.)

RACHEL: So am I in this? Am I in your...journal?

NICHOLAS: You're all over it, Rachel. It starts with you.

(A moment. Then NICHOLAS exits. RACHEL goes to the window and closes it. The sound of the rain dies down. She goes back to the table and sits down. She lights up a cigarette. She opens the plastic bag and a threadbare book with loose pages spills out. She opens it. She begins to read aloud.)

RACHEL: From the diary of Nicholas J Barnes. This act of documentation is new to me. I've never kept a journal before. Never been much on self-examination, I suppose. So I don't really know who I'm talking to. Or what I hope to accomplish by keeping these notes. But a voice inside my head says: Do it. Commit it to paper. Commit it to memory. Remember, Nicholas. Remember.

Scene 2

(The sound of more thunder. RACHEL turns a page in the journal. She takes a drag on her cigarette and continues to read aloud.)

RACHEL: It's a weekday night in early September. I make my way through L A X towards my destination. The bar outside the entrance to the airport terminal. A watering hole that serves over-priced drinks to people on the run.

(We hear the sound of an airplane flying overhead.)

RACHEL: I order a Scotch and throw it back. I order another. I move to a table and check the time hoping that I'm not too late.

(There is a shift in the lighting now as NICHOLAS *enters wearing a suit and tie. He carries a drink with him that he puts down on a table. He checks his watch. He remains on his feet. The sounds of airport traffic and flight announcements are heard and underscore the scene. The understanding is that we have moved back in time and that the events of the play will proceed within the confines of the attic. We will forget that we are in an attic as this space becomes the playing area for our story. The antique furniture and heirlooms will become our props. The changes in locale will happen through the lighting and sound and the movement of the characters who will come and go through spaces between the walls. The action is continuous. Almost dreamlike. One scene spills over right into the next.)*

RACHEL: I'm surrounded by the rush of humanity. The endless flow of parties in transition. Of people between places.

(A DERELICT *enters carrying an old traveling bag. He sees* NICHOLAS. *He slowly crosses to him.)*

RACHEL: And then I see him. A derelict shuffling through the crowd. His clothes are weathered. His shoes, worn. His expression, blank. He seems to be coming towards me. Seems to want something. Then he stops.

(The DERELICT *stops.)*

RACHEL: And he stands there. Staring at me. Not moving. Not saying anything. I attempt to ignore him. I take another drink. I turn away. Then he starts talking nonsense.

DERELICT: Next in line.

NICHOLAS: What?

DERELICT: You're next in line.

NICHOLAS: I don't know what you're talking about.

DERELICT: No. But you will. Soon.

RACHEL: And with that the man simply turns and walks away.

(The DERELICT *exits.)*

RACHEL: I watch him depart. Watch him as he disappears back into the crowd. I shudder and don't know why.

*(*RACHEL *puts out her cigarette. She rises and puts the journal in her pocket. She walks to a corner of the stage and stares at* NICHOLAS.*)*

RACHEL: Nicholas?

*(*NICHOLAS *doesn't hear* RACHEL.*)*

RACHEL: Nicholas Barnes?

*(*NICHOLAS *turns and sees* RACHEL. *A moment)*

NICHOLAS: Rachel?

RACHEL: Yeah.

NICHOLAS: Oh, my gosh. My gosh, look at you. You look—

RACHEL: Nervous?

NICHOLAS: No.

RACHEL: Exhausted?

NICHOLAS: No, no, you look good. Honestly. How was your flight?

RACHEL: Fine. We were late getting out of San Francisco. I thought I might miss you.

NICHOLAS: I got a table.

(NICHOLAS *and* RACHEL *move to the table. He pulls out a chair for her and she sits.*)

NICHOLAS: Is this okay? I didn't—

RACHEL: No, this is fine. I…I can only stay for a few minutes. But I appreciate your coming.

NICHOLAS: Hey, I'm glad you called. Really. How did you find me? *(He sits.)*

RACHEL: It's wasn't easy. But I remembered a name. Your school.

NICHOLAS: Law school?

RACHEL: High school. They told me where you went to college. I talked to someone on the alumni association.

NICHOLAS: They're always sending me crap.

RACHEL: They knew where you were.

NICHOLAS: Of course.

RACHEL: I don't get to Los Angeles that often. Like never. And when I found out I was going to have this layover—

NICHOLAS: Can I get you a drink?

RACHEL: No, thanks. *(She pulls out a pack of cigarettes, lights one up, and chain-smokes her way through the following conversation.)*

NICHOLAS: So how long has it been since we've actually—?

RACHEL: Seen each other?

NICHOLAS: Yeah.

RACHEL: Seventeen years.

NICHOLAS: Seventeen years?

RACHEL: You don't remember?

NICHOLAS: No, no, I do. I just...thought I'd seen you since then.

RACHEL: It was the summer before Grandma died.

NICHOLAS: Right.

RACHEL: The last summer.

NICHOLAS: Got it.

RACHEL: I mean, the last time my family ever made it back east.

NICHOLAS: Mine, too.

RACHEL: Yeah?

NICHOLAS: Oh, yeah. As memory serves. Well, obviously, mine's not serving too well. *(He laughs.)*

RACHEL: So how are you doing?

NICHOLAS: Me? I'm good. What do I mean good? I'm great. Over-worked, under-paid, and up to my knees in debt, but there it is. The white man's burden.

RACHEL: So you're practicing law?

NICHOLAS: I'm with one of the top firms downtown. On the track to an associate post. If everything goes according to plan.

RACHEL: Isn't that something?

NICHOLAS: Oh, yeah, believe me, it *is* something. I'm only hoping it happens before the end.

RACHEL: The end of what?

NICHOLAS: You know, the millennium. The big changeover. 1999 into the twenty-first century. The American century, right? I mean, who knows when we'll get another? So I'd like something to celebrate. Between now and then. And you?

RACHEL: What?

NICHOLAS: Do you have any plans for the end of the decade?

RACHEL: Uh, no. Nothing in particular.

NICHOLAS: Okay. *(Pause)* So tell me about San Francisco. What do you do there?

RACHEL: Artwork. Commercial artwork. Freelance, mostly, because I...can't stand to be around the same people for more than a month or two.

NICHOLAS: Hey, I know what that's like.

RACHEL: I mean, I live alone.

NICHOLAS: So you're not married?

RACHEL: No.

NICHOLAS: Boyfriend?

RACHEL: Not at present.

NICHOLAS: Are you sure you don't want a drink?

RACHEL: I'm sure.

(Pause)

NICHOLAS: Hey, how's your brother?

RACHEL: My brother? *(Pause)* I guess you don't know.

NICHOLAS: What?

RACHEL: He...killed himself. Almost a year ago.

NICHOLAS: No.

RACHEL: They found him in an empty room above some bar in New Orleans. He'd been on a bender. Bought a gun. And...it happened.

NICHOLAS: I'm sorry.

RACHEL: Well, it's what he wanted, I guess.

NICHOLAS: Does anybody know why?

RACHEL: No. I mean, he had this successful medical practice going for awhile. And then the bottom dropped out of everything. He lost his office. His house. One thing led to another. *(Pause)* He called me once. From a payphone out on some highway. He was high. On painkillers, I think. And he said, "Rachel, we are all guilty." Then he laughed. And then he hung up.

NICHOLAS: Guilty?

RACHEL: Yeah.

NICHOLAS: Of what?

RACHEL: He didn't say. *(Pause)* I was the next of kin, so I got to identify his body.

NICHOLAS: I'm surprised.

RACHEL: Why?

NICHOLAS: Well, I would have thought that was something your father could have taken care of.

RACHEL: My father? *(Pause)* You don't know?

NICHOLAS: Know what?

RACHEL: My father's dead, Nicholas. He's been dead for almost six years now.

NICHOLAS: No.

RACHEL: And my mom, too.

NICHOLAS: You're kidding me?

RACHEL: I thought you knew.

NICHOLAS: How would I know?

RACHEL: Well, I thought your dad would have told you.

(Pause)

NICHOLAS: My dad's gone, Rachel.

RACHEL: He—?

NICHOLAS: A while ago.

RACHEL: When?

NICHOLAS: Well, about the same time I was getting out of law school. What's it been? Seven, eight years?

RACHEL: And your mother?

NICHOLAS: She— *(Pause)* I lost her a few months later.

RACHEL: Oh, God.

NICHOLAS: I would have let you know.

RACHEL: Oh, my God.

NICHOLAS: But I didn't know how to contact you. Where you were living.

RACHEL: No.

NICHOLAS: Last I knew your family was in, what? Seattle?

RACHEL: And you were in Phoenix.

NICHOLAS: That's right. And then—

RACHEL: We all lost touch.

NICHOLAS: We did.

RACHEL: Our families sort of splintered apart.

NICHOLAS: Well—

RACHEL: I mean, our fathers stopped talking.

NICHOLAS: I suppose that's true.

RACHEL: After she died.

NICHOLAS: She?

RACHEL: Grandma. *(Pause)* I remember the morning he got the phone call. He'd been out east for a few days with her and with your father, I think. And when he got home he and my mom had this huge argument. And then that call came. And he let us know that she was gone. And then he went away. To the funeral. Without us. *(Pause)* Do you remember any of this?

NICHOLAS: Some. The call. My dad's reaction.

RACHEL: How did he react?

NICHOLAS: How? Well, he— *(Pause)* Didn't.

RACHEL: How do you mean?

NICHOLAS: There was no reaction. He told us about it. Then he packed his suitcase and hit the road.

RACHEL: Did you go to the funeral?

NICHOLAS: I— *(Pause)* Well, I was in school at the time. And it would have meant missing my classes. My studies. So...no. No, I didn't go.

RACHEL: Me neither.

NICHOLAS: And, really, would it have mattered? To her? She barely knew us.

RACHEL: She loved you.

NICHOLAS: She what?

RACHEL: Adored you. "My Nicky." I can still see her running her hands through your hair.

NICHOLAS: I have no recollection of this.

RACHEL: Do you know how she died?

NICHOLAS: Do I?

RACHEL: Yeah.

NICHOLAS: Well, I— *(Pause)* I was told that she died... quietly. In her sleep.

RACHEL: That's what I was told, too. *(Pause)* I brought you this photograph. *(She reaches into her pocket and pulls it out.)* Look. *(She hands it to him.)* This was taken

outside the farmhouse the last time we were all
together.

NICHOLAS: Well, well. What do you know? The whole
brood.

RACHEL: Yeah, the entire family. *(Pause)* Do you
remember that place?

NICHOLAS: Sort of. I remember the event. The annual
pilgrimage to Grandma's farm.

RACHEL: I loved that old house. The feel of it. The
smells. And that attic upstairs where we used to knock
around. Used to sleep. *(Pause)* Sometimes there in the
dark I'd wake up. I could hear the sounds of people
downstairs in the kitchen arguing. I wondered if you
could hear them, too.

NICHOLAS: I might have.

RACHEL: My dad was shouting. Your dad was
shouting. Grandma was carrying on. I never really
knew what they were all fighting about, did you?

NICHOLAS: Well, no. Not really. I suppose there were…
problems.

RACHEL: What kind of problems?

NICHOLAS: Well, cash flow. Financial. Maybe.

RACHEL: But specifically?

NICHOLAS: I…I don't know.

RACHEL: No. They never said. And lately… *(Pause)*
It's like that again. I mean, I can't sleep. I wake up at
three A M. What they call the midnight of the soul.
When everything you believe is held up to question.
When there are no absolute truths and all the world is
suspect. And it's like I can still hear them in my head.
Downstairs. Arguing. *(Pause)* Has anything…?

NICHOLAS: Yeah?

RACHEL: It's just that there's been this series of...
incidents. I don't really know what else to call them.
Random events.

NICHOLAS: Like what?

RACHEL: Things disappearing. Or being taken away.
Phone calls. The sense that something is out there.
Some person or other.

NICHOLAS: Who?

RACHEL: I don't know. *(Pause)* But I can't get rid of
the feeling that I'm being followed. That everything is
starting to slip into the past. That maybe, possibly—
(Pause) Someone is out to get me. *(She laughs.)* So.
(Pause) So you have no idea what I'm talking about.

NICHOLAS: Rachel, are you alright?

RACHEL: Not really. *(She laughs.)* I have to catch that
flight.

(RACHEL *stands and* NICHOLAS *does, too.)*

NICHOLAS: I'll walk with you.

RACHEL: No, it's alright.

NICHOLAS: Where are you going?

RACHEL: To the gate.

NICHOLAS: Yeah, I know, but where are you flying to?

RACHEL: Oh. Back home. San Francisco.

NICHOLAS: But— *(Pause)* I thought you just came from
there.

RACHEL: Yeah, I...I did, but, uh...

(Pause)

NICHOLAS: I don't understand.

RACHEL: Well, there's nothing to understand. Nothing
that I can...I have to go. I'll call you from the, uh...

well, when I get home. Or soon. I promise. I…I only…
(Pause) Wanted to check in.

(A moment. Then RACHEL *turns and exits.* NICHOLAS
*notices the photograph that she has left on the table. He picks
it up and calls after her.)*

NICHOLAS: Rachel?

(But RACHEL *is gone.* NICHOLAS *looks at the photograph in
his hand.)*

Scene 3

*(*MARTIN *enters and observes* NICHOLAS.*)*

MARTIN: Good morning.

*(*NICHOLAS *is snapped from his reverie. He puts the
photograph in his pocket. We are in his law office.)*

NICHOLAS: Oh, hey, Martin, how's it going?

MARTIN: Going well. Going very well. 'Course, it could
be going better. I could be you. I could be the crown
prince standing on top of the world taking a leak on
those less fortunate.

NICHOLAS: Nothing is certain until it happens.

MARTIN: Oh, listen to this. Mr Slick. Mr Super-
Imposed-Modesty-Himself. Don't, Nick. It doesn't
become you. Everyone knows that you're on the short
list. And most people in the office think that for once
Metzger and Neidhardt might actually have made a
good decision. 'Course, I'm not one of them.

*(*NICHOLAS *laughs.)*

MARTIN: Promise me something.

NICHOLAS: What's that?

MARTIN: When you get to be an associate, try to remember all the little people who made you what you are today.

NICHOLAS: Hey, I'll try, but the truth is I did it all myself.

MARTIN: That's more like it. *(He finds a comfortable spot and sits.)*

NICHOLAS: Have a seat.

MARTIN: Love to.

(NICHOLAS moves to another table and begins rifling through some papers.)

MARTIN: So how was your date last night?

NICHOLAS: Not a date, Martin. A meeting. Someone I hadn't seen in a long time.

MARTIN: Oh?

NICHOLAS: My cousin.

MARTIN: Cute?

NICHOLAS: Pardon me?

MARTIN: Is she cute?

NICHOLAS: I will never introduce you.

MARTIN: Coward.

(NICHOLAS picks up a slip of paper from off of the table.)

NICHOLAS: "Call Amelia."

MARTIN: Okay. What's her number?

NICHOLAS: No, it's just a note. Who puts this stuff here?

MARTIN: New receptionist. Does the same thing with my calls. Who's Amelia?

NICHOLAS: I don't know. I don't know anyone by that name.

MARTIN: Me neither. No message?

NICHOLAS: Nope. *(Pause)* My grandmother was named Amelia.

MARTIN: Oh, yeah?

NICHOLAS: Yeah.

MARTIN: I like older women.

NICHOLAS: Martin—

MARTIN: I'm kidding.

NICHOLAS: She's dead!

MARTIN: Probably not her then.

*(*NICHOLAS *laughs, crumples up the paper, and tosses it to one side.)*

NICHOLAS: She was always an enigma wrapped up in a what-do-you-call-it.

MARTIN: How so?

NICHOLAS: Well, she struggled all her life trying to sustain this property in the middle of nowhere, Pennsylvania. This piece of land that produced a few crops. Nothing to write home about. But she stayed there anyway, working it, relentlessly, like the place actually meant something to her. Then her family moved on. She got older. And she died.

MARTIN: Sad. Sad story.

NICHOLAS: Yeah, well, don't let it break you up, okay?

MARTIN: Me?

NICHOLAS: Do you ever do any work around here?

MARTIN: God, no. That would completely ruin my reputation. I only came by to deliver a message.

NICHOLAS: I'm listening.

MARTIN: Metzger wants to see you.

NICHOLAS: When?

MARTIN: This afternoon. Who knows, Nicko? This could be your lucky day.

Scene 4

(LOUISE *enters as* MARTIN *exits. She is wearing running clothes and is clearly out of breath. She begins to undress.* NICHOLAS *mixes himself a drink. We are now in his apartment.*)

NICHOLAS: So I'm sitting there. And Metzger is telling me nothing from the expression on his face. I mean, the last time I saw this guy smile was the day he found out how much money his mother had left him in her will. Then he leans back and says, "Nicholas, Harrison Seitz is one of my oldest friends. He also happens to be the C E O of Bethesda Oil and one of this city's wealthiest men. That aside, it seems that his stockholders have brought a suit against him and he wants us to represent him. Now, ordinarily, I'd give an assignment of this magnitude to Paxton or Ross." Ross, what a total loser. "But, Harrison has asked for somebody younger. Fresher. More energetic. And I recommended you. Now, Nicholas, it hardly needs to be said," but, of course, he says it anyway, "If you do this right, you'll make me proud. And when I'm proud, I tend to reward."

LOUISE: Uh-huh.

NICHOLAS: That's a direct quote, Louise.

LOUISE: So that means—

NICHOLAS: It means he's practically handing me the partnership on a platter.

LOUISE: That's great. That's really great. Good for you.

NICHOLAS: Yes. Yes, it *is* good for me. It's goddamn *great* for me!

LOUISE: Congratulations.

NICHOLAS: I'm supposed to hand off the rest of my cases. To concentrate on this and nothing else. God, I am so charged!

LOUISE: I can tell.

NICHOLAS: Do you want a drink?

LOUISE: Can't. I have to be in class by six-thirty. Tonight we study reverse-trend economics. Whatever the hell that is. What are you going to do?

NICHOLAS: Prepare. Go over my reports. My first meeting with the man is a week from Thursday.

LOUISE: You work too hard.

NICHOLAS: Hey, I've never denied it, but what else is there?

(LOUISE *kisses* NICHOLAS *seductively.*)

NICHOLAS: Oh, yeah, now I remember.

LOUISE: Want to buy some love?

NICHOLAS: How much?

LOUISE: Fifty, please.

(NICHOLAS *smiles. He hands* LOUISE *some money. She kisses him again.*)

LOUISE: I love you.

(NICHOLAS *laughs.* LOUISE *exits, but continues to talk from offstage.*)

LOUISE: I missed you last night.

NICHOLAS: Yeah, sorry, I was so late.

LOUISE: Did you find her? Did you find your cousin?

NICHOLAS: I did.

LOUISE: And? Did you have a nice time?

NICHOLAS: Sort of. Actually, no. It was a little...odd.

LOUISE: How's that?

NICHOLAS: Well, I think there was something eating away at her. Something that she wanted to talk about, but couldn't. And then, in the middle of the conversation, she simply got up and left. She said she had to catch her flight, but it turns out she was going back the way she came. So there was no real reason to come here at all.

LOUISE: Hmm.

NICHOLAS: Except to see me.

LOUISE: And who'd want to do that?

(NICHOLAS *laughs and pulls the photograph out of his pocket and looks at it.*)

NICHOLAS: She left me with this picture.

LOUISE: Of what?

NICHOLAS: Me and my family. When I was a kid.

(LOUISE *enters wearing a blouse and trousers. She is combing out her hair.*)

LOUISE: Let's see.

NICHOLAS: No.

LOUISE: Oh, come on.

NICHOLAS: Why?

LOUISE: Because I'm interested.

(NICHOLAS *shows* LOUISE *the photograph.*)

LOUISE: Is that supposed to be you?

NICHOLAS: Ah…yeah.

LOUISE: Well, your ears have certainly gotten smaller.

NICHOLAS: What are you saying?

LOUISE: They're not as large as they once were.

NICHOLAS: You think I had big ears?

LOUISE: Oh, come on, Nick, you look like Dumbo in this picture. *(Pause)* Who's the girl?

NICHOLAS: That's my cousin, Rachel.

LOUISE: And the boy standing next to her?

NICHOLAS: Her brother.

LOUISE: And that's your aunt.

NICHOLAS: Aunt Jacqueline. That's right. The family scandal.

LOUISE: Oh?

NICHOLAS: She had an illegitimate child. A boy. And of course—

LOUISE: It wasn't done back then.

NICHOLAS: No, it wasn't. He's standing right here. My cousin, Eugene. Must have been…what? Seven, eight?

LOUISE: Who's the man standing behind you?

NICHOLAS: That's my dad.

LOUISE: Oh. *(Pause)* You never talk about him.

NICHOLAS: No?

LOUISE: No. *(Pause)* Why is that?

NICHOLAS: Well. *(Pause)* He spent his whole life in sales. Working eighteen hour days for this shipping company. He was their number one man. Always on the go. On the road or in the air. He had this expression. "Nick," he'd say, "He travels fastest who travels alone." And that's exactly what he did. He traveled alone. *(Pause)* One night he was coming back from some out of town presentation. He'd just lost this major client who he'd been working with for years. There were money problems at home. Debts he'd accumulated. And he was spent. Physically exhausted. Anyway, he was sitting in this airport in Minneapolis. And he got up out of his chair and walked out onto

the tarmac. And this plane had just touched down,
see. And the propeller was still in motion. Still going
around. And he... *(Pause)* He walked right into it.
Right into the propeller. He didn't stop.

LOUISE: My God.

NICHOLAS: Yeah. No explanation. He just...walked into
it.

(Pause)

LOUISE: And your mom?

(NICHOLAS *downs his drink. A moment)*

NICHOLAS: She started to lose it after that. Started
taking pills. Sleeping pills. One night she took too
many. *(Pause)* And she never woke up.

LOUISE: God. *(Pause)* I gotta go. *(She grabs a set of
keys of a table and starts to exit.)* Oh, I knew there was
something else.

NICHOLAS: What's that?

LOUISE: The mortgage company called.

NICHOLAS: I already sent the check.

LOUISE: It bounced.

NICHOLAS: It what?

LOUISE: The check bounced.

NICHOLAS: That's not possible.

LOUISE: Better call the bank.

NICHOLAS: It's their mistake.

LOUISE: Hey, whatever. It's your condo, babe. I only
live here. *(She kisses him.)* Later.

Scene 5

(MARTIN *enters as* LOUISE *exits. We are again in*
NICHOLAS'*s office.*)

NICHOLAS: How could that be?

MARTIN: I don't know.

NICHOLAS: How could they let that much money fall
out of my account? *Any* money fall out of my account?

MARTIN: Did you go to the bank?

NICHOLAS: Oh, yeah. I spent the entire morning with
those clowns. I said, "Look, I've got four thousand
in checking, five thousand in savings, and I recently
turned over some C Ds worth fifteen grand."

MARTIN: You don't need to go into the specifics.

NICHOLAS: "Now, given those numbers as my net
worth, how could one check for twelve hundred
dollars have bounced?"

MARTIN: And they said—?

NICHOLAS: "As of two days ago it wouldn't have.
But during the last forty-eight hours, Mr Barnes, you
have been making a series of transactions that have
completely liquidated your assets."

MARTIN: You what?

NICHOLAS: Withdrawals. Electronic withdrawals. I'm
completely wiped out.

MARTIN: And you don't remember doing this?

NICHOLAS: No, I don't…I didn't make them, Martin!
Somebody else did!

MARTIN: How?

NICHOLAS: I don't know how. They got access to my
I D. My info.

MARTIN: So what are you going to do?

NICHOLAS: Shut down the accounts. Claim fraud. File a suit that'll bust open their federal reserves.

MARTIN: Definitely.

NICHOLAS: I mean, Jesus Christ, who would do something like this?

MARTIN: Someone who needed the money?

NICHOLAS: Yeah, well, that narrows it down.

MARTIN: So how are you sitting?

NICHOLAS: What do you mean?

MARTIN: I mean, in the meantime, let me loan you some cash.

NICHOLAS: No, it's alright. Louise has got me covered.

MARTIN: Nice girl. She got any sisters?

NICHOLAS: Martin?

MARTIN: Yeah?

NICHOLAS: Do me a favor.

MARTIN: Okay.

NICHOLAS: Go away.

MARTIN: Why?

NICHOLAS: Because I'm about to fucking break something!

MARTIN: Gone. Out of here. Hey, listen, Metzger wants the files.

NICHOLAS: The what?

MARTIN: The files. On the other cases you were handling. He wants to bring the rest of us peons up to speed.

NICHOLAS: I sent them out yesterday.

MARTIN: You did?

NICHOLAS: Interoffice mail.

MARTIN: Well, he never got them.

Scene 6

(LOUISE *enters as* MARTIN *exits.* NICHOLAS *turns to her. We are again in his apartment. She is sorting out laundry, separating his from hers.)*

NICHOLAS: Listen to me.

LOUISE: I am.

NICHOLAS: The files are lost. The paperwork's missing. No one at the firm has a clue.

LOUISE: Okay.

NICHOLAS: But I'm being cool, because I've got everything backed up.

LOUISE: Uh-huh.

NICHOLAS: I go to the computer. I put in the password.

LOUISE: And?

NICHOLAS: Gone. *(Pause)* The files are gone, Louise.

LOUISE: I heard you the first time.

NICHOLAS: Someone got in there. Deleted my notes. Erased my research.

LOUISE: Are you sure that—?

NICHOLAS: What?

LOUISE: Well, the fact is, you stare at that computer all day long.

NICHOLAS: Are you saying that I could have somehow done this and not remembered?

LOUISE: All it takes is one naughty finger.

NICHOLAS: You're not listening.

LOUISE: I had this friend who went on this radical diet plan. She lost fifteen pounds in two weeks. Then one night she dreams that she's eating an entire pumpernickel loaf. She wakes up in the kitchen staring into the refrigerator. There's an empty plastic bag in her hand and breadcrumbs all over the floor.

NICHOLAS: Here's the difference. I'm not asleep.

LOUISE: And you're not overweight. *(Pause)* Do you want to rent a movie? *(Pause)* Do you want to go out for Thai food?

NICHOLAS: What I want is an explanation. Some reasonable facsimile of cause and effect.

LOUISE: Hey, shit happens.

NICHOLAS: Shit. Happens. *(Pause)* Thank you, Louise. I will attempt to console myself with that incredibly small wisdom.

LOUISE: Look, Nick, it's like this. You put a pencil down on one side of the room. A minute later it turns up somewhere else.

NICHOLAS: A pencil? Louise, I'm talking about seventy-five pages of notes. Tens of thousands of dollars.

LOUISE: It's a process of extension.

NICHOLAS: Do you think I'm capable of doing these things and not remembering? *(Pause)* Do you?

LOUISE: I don't like being put under the gun this way.

NICHOLAS: No. I want to know. You observe me everyday.

LOUISE: Nicholas—

NICHOLAS: I hesitate to say that you might even know me.

LOUISE: I—

NICHOLAS: ANSWER ME!

LOUISE: Yes! Alright? Yes! When you talk to me like this. When you come at me like *I'm* the enemy. Yes, I think you could have done all these things and more. You could have murdered someone for all I know. Now will you please lighten up? If not for your own sake, then at least for mine. I'm sorry about the money. I'm sorry about your files. But it's not my fault.

NICHOLAS: I never said that it was.

LOUISE: Yeah, well, please, *please* try to remember that. *(She exits. A moment. Then she walks back on stage.)* And another thing, while we're airing our differences, when your girlfriends call here and I answer the phone, could you ask them to please have the decency to hang up?

NICHOLAS: Somebody called?

LOUISE: Yes. Somebody called.

NICHOLAS: Did they leave a message?

LOUISE: No. No message. Just her name.

NICHOLAS: Her name?

LOUISE: Yes. *(Pause)* Amelia.

Scene 7

(RACHEL enters as LOUISE exits. The journal is in her hand along with a cigarette. She reads aloud.)

RACHEL: I sleep fitfully that night. And for several nights thereafter. I dream of Rachel. Standing at the edge of my delirium. A book is in her hands. Maybe it's this one. The journal I've started to keep for reasons I don't understand.

(NICHOLAS sits at a table.)

RACHEL: Over the course of the next few days I attempt to complete my research on Bethesda Oil. I can't afford to fail in this matter. To fail the firm. Or myself. Then one night I'm alone in the apartment. Working late. The world is still. Almost serene. Suddenly I stop. *(He does.)*

RACHEL: I stare out into the street. No reason. No reason at all.

(The DERELICT *enters and moves into a pool of light. He stops. He looks at* NICHOLAS.*)*

RACHEL: And I see him. In the streetlight underneath my window. Looking up at my apartment. Looking up at me. I blink. And he's gone.

(The DERELICT *turns and exits.* NICHOLAS *remains staring at the space that he has occupied.)*

RACHEL: I look at the phone. I hesitate. I pick it up.

*(*NICHOLAS *does.)*

RACHEL: I dial.

*(*NICHOLAS *does.)*

RACHEL: And then I hear a voice saying: Operator.

NICHOLAS: Yes, I'm looking for a listing on a Rachel Barnes somewhere in the Bay Area.

RACHEL: Barnes?

NICHOLAS: B-A-R-N-E-S. First name, Rachel.

RACHEL: Hold, please. *(Pause)* I'm sorry. I show no listing.

NICHOLAS: No listing? Are you sure about that? No initial R Barnes?

RACHEL: I show no listing, sir. Not in the Bay Area.

NICHOLAS: Alright.

RACHEL: I hang up.

(NICHOLAS *does.*)

RACHEL: I look back out into the night. I think of
the derelict standing below. A strange coincidence.
Nothing more. I get up.

(NICHOLAS *does.*)

RACHEL: I move to the center of the room. I lie down on
the floor. And I drift off into the momentary bliss of a
pure and soundless sleep.

(NICHOLAS *lies down on the floor and closes his eyes.*
RACHEL *leaves the stage. Silence*)

Scene 8

(MARTIN *enters. He looks down at* NICHOLAS *sleeping on
the floor. We are once again in* NICHOLAS'*s office.*)

MARTIN: Hey, sport. Looks like I caught you sleeping
on the job.

(NICHOLAS *stirs.*)

MARTIN: On the floor.

(NICHOLAS *looks up.*)

NICHOLAS: What? Oh. Oh, I…uh…oh, man.

MARTIN: No need to explain.

NICHOLAS: I just…I put my head down for a minute
and—

MARTIN: Lights out. I know how it is. Let's get out of
here. Get some air. Lunch is on me.

NICHOLAS: What time is it?

MARTIN: Time? Who cares? We're young. We're
working men. The world is our massage parlor. Time is
a magazine. Twelve-thirty.

NICHOLAS: Twelve-thirty?

(NICHOLAS *looks at his watch.*)

MARTIN: So how'd the meeting go this morning?

NICHOLAS: The...meeting?

MARTIN: Wasn't today your first face to face with Harrison Seitz? *(Pause)* Hello?

NICHOLAS: Oh, Christ.

(NICHOLAS *hurriedly gets up, goes to a table, and grabs a pile of papers.*)

MARTIN: Oh, God, Nick.

NICHOLAS: Do me a favor. Call ahead. Say something.

MARTIN: What should I say?

NICHOLAS: I don't know. Anything. Tell them there was a death in the family.

MARTIN: I may not be lying.

NICHOLAS: Christ!

(NICHOLAS *rushes off.* MARTIN *watches him go. He shakes his head.*)

Scene 9

(HARRISON SEITZ *enters as* MARTIN *exits. He sits. We are in his office suite in the Bethesda Oil Building. A moment. Then* NICHOLAS *comes running onstage. He stops.*)

NICHOLAS: Mr Seitz, I am so terribly—

SEITZ: Do you know the history behind Bethesda Oil, Mr Barnes?

NICHOLAS: Uh... *(He shuffles through the papers in his hand.)* I believe I have it here somewhere.

SEITZ: Sit down. No, actually, this is worth standing for. Stay as you are.

(Pause)

NICHOLAS: Okay.

SEITZ: It was Nineteen Sixty-Seven. I was working
for one of our chief competitors. My job consisted of
setting up meetings with potential clients. Going to
their place of business. And waiting. *(Pause)* Waiting
for the vice-president. Waiting for the district manager.
Waiting for the secretary to return from lunch. Do you
follow?

NICHOLAS: I—

SEITZ: One week I traveled halfway across the country
to meet with a man I'd been scheduled to see for six
months. I'd been up half the night preparing. I'd worn
my best suit. I'd spent the last dollar in my pocket on
a shoeshine and a manicure. And I arrived at his office
several minutes before our appointment only to be told
that he'd been called out of town unexpectedly and
wouldn't be returning for several days. *(Pause)* What
do you think I did?

NICHOLAS: Well—

SEITZ: I made a decision. In that instant. I would take
control of my destiny. I would build my *own* company
from the ground floor up. I would leave this no man's
land of waiting behind. I would not wait. I would no
longer wait.

(Pause)

NICHOLAS: I think I understand and again—

SEITZ: Now, today, Bethesda Oil is something of
a novelty in the business world. We honor our
commitment to our customers. To our employees.
And to our government. We do this because we are
responsible to one man. His word is his deed. And I *am*
that man. *(Pause)* A suit's been brought against me by
my own stockholders. I've been accused of trading on

inside information. It's absurd. A falsehood. A lie. So
what do I do? Where do I turn? *(Pause)* Yes?

NICHOLAS: You called our firm.

SEITZ: I go to Wendall Metzger. A confidant. A friend.
I say I need your assistance. He says I'll send you
Nicholas Barnes. A gifted, young attorney almost
certain to make associate partner by the end of the
year. He's thorough. Professional. Relentless in his
pursuit of excellence. The fair-haired boy of the firm. A
man most capable. And, oh, yes— *(Pause)* Punctual.

NICHOLAS: Mr Seitz, I can take care of you. I've been
through your reports. I've studied your records. I have
extensively researched the legal aspects of this case.
You have done nothing wrong. And I can prove that. I
can prove that in a court of law.

*(A moment. SEITZ stares at NICHOLAS. Then he leans back
in his chair.)*

SEITZ: Let's get started.

Scene 10

*(The sound of loud music overtakes the stage. MARTIN
enters with two drinks. SEITZ rises and exits. MARTIN hands
one of the drinks to NICHOLAS. We are in a sports bar.)*

NICHOLAS: Oh, man, I almost blew it. Almost bottomed
out big time. Goodbye, career. Whoosh! Down the
proverbial toilet.

MARTIN: You are one lucky son of a bitch.

NICHOLAS: Tell me about it.

MARTIN: I thought you were prepared for this thing.

NICHOLAS: I was. I don't know what happened. I lost
track of the days.

MARTIN: Well, staple a calendar to your head, okay?

NICHOLAS: I haven't been sleeping well.

MARTIN: Hey, nobody sleeps well, but even insomniacs cover their ass.

NICHOLAS: Yeah, well, thanks for all the sympathetic camaraderie.

MARTIN: Nick, Nicko, Nickelodeon, can I say something?

NICHOLAS: No.

MARTIN: You don't look so good.

NICHOLAS: What are you talking about?

MARTIN: What I'm talking about is the fact that you appear to have been hit by a bus and dragged twenty blocks. Buddy, I got to ask you something. Are you on drugs?

NICHOLAS: No.

MARTIN: Would you like to be? *(Pause)* I'm kidding.

NICHOLAS: I told you—

MARTIN: I know. Too many late nights. Too little time in the hot tub. But do yourself a favor. Snap out of it.

NICHOLAS: Look, I pulled it off, alright? The man trusts me. I told him he was innocent.

MARTIN: Is he?

NICHOLAS: How the fuck should I know?

MARTIN: Spoken like a true professional. Listen, I'm going to pay for these drinks. Then I'm going to get two more.

NICHOLAS: I'm fine.

MARTIN: Not for you, studley. I see something at the end of the bar with my name on it. Hey, I'm amazed

that you pulled it off. Really. You lead a charmed life.
It makes me sick. I'll see you in the morning.

(MARTIN *takes* NICHOLAS's *glass with him as he dances*
offstage. The music fades with him.)

Scene 11

(RACHEL *enters with the journal as* MARTIN *exits.*
NICHOLAS *rises and moves across the stage. As he does the*
DERELICT *enters. He walks to the center of the stage, reaches*
into his bag, pulls out an object wrapped up in a cloth. He
uncovers the cloth. He is holding up a silver box. He stares
at it for a moment. Then he bends down and carefully
places it on the floor. This all happens simultaneously with
RACHEL's *narrative.*)

RACHEL: I drive home that night feeling no pain.
The city seems boundless. Limitless. Each freeway is
another path. Each boulevard, another possibility. For
the first time in several weeks, I find myself thinking
that I am somehow back on track. That all of this
has been a bad dream that I am finally coming out
of. I enter my building and climb the stairs. I walk
down the hallway. And I discover the door to my
apartment...open. Wide open.

(*The* DERELICT *leaves the stage and crosses in front of*
NICHOLAS's *path.* NICHOLAS *does not see him go. He*
stands staring into the room.)

NICHOLAS: Louise? (*Pause*) Hello? (*He moves slowly*
through the room and then toward the center of the stage.)

RACHEL: I wander through the rooms. Nothing's
missing. Everything's as I left it. I come to the living
room. A sliver of light from the street hits the floor.
And I see something gleaming.

(NICHOLAS *bends down and picks up the box. He opens it. A slim melody leaks out. A melody of another time and place. Finally it runs down. He closes the box.* LOUISE *enters behind him. She stops. She looks down.*)

LOUISE:What are you doing?

(NICHOLAS *turns to* LOUISE.)

NICHOLAS: God, you frightened me.

LOUISE: *I* frightened *you*? I come home and find the front door open and you standing here in the dark holding a…what is that?

NICHOLAS: It's a music box. It used to belong to my grandmother. When she was a girl.

LOUISE: Oh. *(Pause)* What's it doing here?

NICHOLAS: I don't know. I walked in and found it on the floor. The door was open. The lights were out.

LOUISE: Uh-huh. *(Pause)* Are you saying that someone broke into the apartment?

NICHOLAS: I'm not sure. I…I guess so.

LOUISE: You guess so? Nick, is anything missing?

NICHOLAS: I don't think so. I think they came here to leave…this.

LOUISE: They? Who? Who are you talking about?

NICHOLAS: I… *(Pause)* I don't know.

LOUISE: Oh, Jesus, Nicholas, pardon me, but life is starting to get a little weird around here. I don't know how to say this in a nice way. I think you need to talk to somebody.

NICHOLAS: Who? *(Pause)* Who would I talk to?

(LOUISE *stares at him. Then she turns and exits.* NICHOLAS *crosses to a chair and sits. He closes his eyes.*)

RACHEL: I can't say for sure what happened next. I sat down to think and fell asleep. I dreamt of fields filled with sunlight. And airplanes. And a cousin I couldn't find.

(The telephone starts to ring. NICHOLAS wakes up.)

RACHEL: Then I'm suddenly awake. I look at my watch.

(NICHOLAS does.)

RACHEL: It is four minutes past three o'clock in the morning. The midnight of the soul. I hesitate. Then I answer the phone.

(NICHOLAS lifts up the phone and speaks into it.)

NICHOLAS: Yes?

RACHEL: This is a collect call from Amelia to Nicholas Barnes. Will you accept the charges? *(Pause)* Will you accept the charges, sir?

(A moment)

NICHOLAS: No.

RACHEL: I hang up.

(NICHOLAS does.)

RACHEL: I don't know why, but I go to the window.

(The DERELICT enters and goes to the pool of light. He turns and looks at NICHOLAS. NICHOLAS looks at him.)

RACHEL: And I see him. Again in the streetlight. Staring up at me. And he's smiling.

(The DERELICT smiles.)

Scene 12

(AMELIA enters from out of the shadows. She is nineteen years old and wears a simple farm dress from another time. She is barefoot. Slowly, she moves across the stage, like a

*spirit, a memory, running her hands over the furniture and
singing a melody without accompaniment other than the
sound of some distant wind. The others do not see her or
acknowledge her, but it is as if her song is somehow locked
into their heads.* RACHEL *exits.)*

AMELIA: In the summer light when the fields are bright
With the marigolds and maize,
We will run with open arms outstretched
To the starting of our days.

(The DERELICT *walks out of the pool of light and leaves the
stage.)*

AMELIA: We will run so fast, we will run so far,
We will set out to begin,
But the summer heat and fields of wheat
Will never come again.

*(*AMELIA *leaves the stage and the sound of the wind fades
with her. She passes* SEITZ *who enters as she exits. We are in
the study of his house.)*

SEITZ: I'm sorry for the interruption. I hate taking calls
at home. But sometimes it can't be helped.

NICHOLAS: Of course.

SEITZ: How was dinner?

NICHOLAS: Excellent.

SEITZ: Where were we?

NICHOLAS: You were telling me about these oil rigs in
Alaska.

SEITZ: Fifteen of them. Bone dry. So the company's lost
a good deal of money.

NICHOLAS: And when was this discovered?

SEITZ: Last spring.

NICHOLAS: But that information wasn't included in
your quarterly report to the stockholders.

SEITZ: That report came out in April. At that point only two of the rigs were dead. The rest were still working well into May.

NICHOLAS: In this report you say that you are optimistic about the state of these rigs.

SEITZ: I'm always optimistic.

NICHOLAS: And yet you sold ten thousand shares of your own stock.

SEITZ: Correct.

NICHOLAS: The day after the first two went dry.

SEITZ: Yes, but, I assure you, these two solitary events are in no way connected.

NICHOLAS: Then why the sale?

SEITZ: I needed the money.

NICHOLAS: Okay. Alright. But on the same day you made this sale you also sold stock in the name of someone else. Someone noted only by the initials J B. *(Pause)* I was wondering who this person might be.

(Pause)

SEITZ: Is this pertinent to my case?

NICHOLAS: It might come up at the deposition.

SEITZ: Well, if you must know, it's an individual who I assist from time to time. An old friend. *(He laughs.)* An ex-wife, actually.

NICHOLAS: Oh.

SEITZ: I still help her with her portfolio.

NICHOLAS: I see.

(Pause)

SEITZ: Something bothering you, Nicholas?

NICHOLAS: No. Well, yes. I suppose. It seems strange. That you would…refer to her this way.

SEITZ: Well, it was my thought that in doing so I could avoid…how should I put it? The possibility of a familial labyrinth.

NICHOLAS: I understand. *(He smiles.)* Interesting choice of words. *(Pause)* So it's not unusual for you to sell a portion of your own stock. Today, last week, last month. That's what I'm trying to get at.

SEITZ: Not at all. It's simply a way of raising capital. Of expanding my resources.

NICHOLAS: Smart. Enterprising, I mean. It…helps to explain your success.

SEITZ: Well, it's what we have to do. We have to go forward. Straight on into the future. Otherwise we become antiques. Souvenirs of another time.

NICHOLAS: Yes. *(Pause)* I'm sorry. You said…?

SEITZ: What?

NICHOLAS: That phrase. The need to go forward. Otherwise we become—?

SEITZ: Antiques. Souvenirs of another time.

(A moment. Time seems to stand still as SEITZ stares at NICHOLAS. We hear the sound of a clock ticking. Then it stops. Silence)

SEITZ: Shall we continue?

NICHOLAS: Of course.

SEITZ: Perhaps you'd like another drink?

NICHOLAS: I…certainly. Thank you.

(SEITZ stands and pours NICHOLAS a drink.)

SEITZ: Tell me, how do you like working for Wendall Metzger?

NICHOLAS: Well, I—

SEITZ: Is he a fair man?

NICHOLAS: Yes. I think so.

(SEITZ hands NICHOLAS the drink.)

SEITZ: And the salary he pays? Is it equitable? I don't mean to pry.

NICHOLAS: No. I mean, yes. It is. By today's standards.

SEITZ: That's good. Life can be a tough enough, eh? For a young man with ambition. Determination. The bills pile up. The paycheck's brought home. And the money disappears. Poof. Who knows where it goes? Suddenly the wolf's at the window.

(Pause)

NICHOLAS: The window.

SEITZ: Yes.

NICHOLAS: What window?

SEITZ: I'm sorry. I meant to say the door. Yes. Suddenly the wolf's at the door. Although, times being what they are, he might also be at the window.

(Another extended moment. Again, we hear the clock. He stares at NICHOLAS.)

NICHOLAS: Yes, I suppose he— *(A moment. Then he stands abruptly.)* You'll have to forgive me.

SEITZ: Nicholas?

NICHOLAS: I'm afraid I have to go. I just remembered…I have to go.

SEITZ: Of course. It's late. You need your sleep.

NICHOLAS: Yes.

SEITZ: I wasn't going to say anything, but you don't look well to me. Not well at all. There's a…weariness to your expression. You're working too hard, I think.

Exhausting yourself. It won't do. Go home, Nicholas.
Get some rest. *(He smiles.)* If you can.

Scene 13

(LOUISE enters as SEITZ exits. NICHOLAS turns to her. We are once again in his apartment.)

NICHOLAS: This man—

LOUISE: Yeah?

NICHOLAS: He knows.

LOUISE: What does he know?

NICHOLAS: Everything.

LOUISE: Must be nice.

NICHOLAS: A souvenir of another time. The wolf outside the window.

LOUISE: Uh-huh.

NICHOLAS: He's talking about the music box.

LOUISE: Really?

NICHOLAS: And the derelict.

LOUISE: What derelict?

NICHOLAS: The one who's been following me. Waiting outside the apartment. The window. That's the wolf. Don't you see?

LOUISE: Not exactly.

NICHOLAS: He's offering me hints, Louise. Clues to stir my interest. Sleep. If you can. What the hell is that? A warning? A threat?

LOUISE: I wouldn't know.

NICHOLAS: It all connects.

LOUISE: To what?

NICHOLAS: The possibility of a familial labyrinth. That's meant for me. I know it.

LOUISE: Ah.

NICHOLAS: It all started with Rachel.

LOUISE: Who?

NICHOLAS: My cousin. I told you. She disappeared.

LOUISE: Of course.

NICHOLAS: And since then everything's come undone. Somebody's been in my files. My bank account. My home. Downstairs in the streetlight. Dead women are calling me on the phone.

LOUISE: Well, at least you've got someone to talk to. *(Pause)* I guess that was sort of a crass thing to say, right?

NICHOLAS: What I'm trying to tell you is that up until tonight I thought I might actually be experiencing some kind of a nervous breakdown.

LOUISE: And you're not?

NICHOLAS: No! Because now I see it. I know what he's concocted.

LOUISE: And that is?

NICHOLAS: The systematic destruction of my life.

LOUISE: Right. *(Pause)* Okay, well, I'm out of here.

NICHOLAS: Where are you going?

LOUISE: I'd rather you didn't know, Nicholas. I don't want you to follow me.

NICHOLAS: You...you're leaving?

LOUISE: Yeah, well. Yes. Yes, that's what I'm doing. If you want to use those words. Alright. I'm leaving. Happy? *(Pause)* I don't know what's going on with you, Nick. And to tell you the truth, I don't want to

know. You used to be a lot of fun to be with. But this
past month you've just become so…self-absorbed.
Dead weight. The king of paranoid delusions.
Somebody's trying to ruin your life? I don't think so.
You've just got to get your shit together. Get help. Get
laid. Get…better. I hope. Well. *(She drops her keys on a
table.)* See ya. *(She exits.)*

Scene 14

*(MARTIN enters. NICHOLAS turns to him. We are once
again in his office.)*

MARTIN: She what?

NICHOLAS: She…she—

MARTIN: She left you?

NICHOLAS: She walked out!

MARTIN: I can't believe this.

NICHOLAS: It just—

MARTIN: Christ!

NICHOLAS: Catches me off balance, because—

MARTIN: You're hurting.

NICHOLAS: The timing—

MARTIN: The timing stinks!

NICHOLAS: But it's alright.

MARTIN: What do you mean, it's alright? It is *not*
alright! It's *all wrong!*

NICHOLAS: It's alright because it makes me stronger.

MARTIN: Listen, Nick. You can always come to my
door. I mean it. My place. The key is yours.

NICHOLAS: It's him and me now.

MARTIN: Right. You and him.

NICHOLAS: It's the only thing that makes sense. He's got the money. The influence.

MARTIN: Sure. *(Pause)* Who're we talking about?

NICHOLAS: Seitz. Harrison Seitz.

MARTIN: Seitz.

NICHOLAS: Yes. *(Pause)* I know what I have to do.

Scene 15

(RACHEL enters with the journal as MARTIN exits.)

RACHEL: I spend the day planning my point of attack. Night comes. And I'm standing outside the urban mansion of my nemesis—Harrison Seitz.

(NICHOLAS moves around to the exterior window and follows the actions as they are described.)

RACHEL: I cut across the lawn and make my way to the side of the house. I'm looking for some way to sever the alarm system when I see a window with a latch that's undone. I pull the frame towards me. The thing comes open. I climb into the house. Slowly. Stealthily.

(NICHOLAS climbs through the frame of the window.)

RACHEL: I'm inside. In his study. I take out a flashlight and shine it through the room.

(NICHOLAS does. The beam from the flashlight cuts across the stage. He shines it through the room.)

RACHEL: I don't know what I'm looking for. Hard evidence. Something concrete to tie him to these crimes.

(NICHOLAS moves about the room.)

RACHEL: I go through photographs. Files. Pieces of trash.

(The beam from the flashlight hits a book on one of the tables.)

RACHEL: And then I see a telephone book. *His* telephone book. With *his* contacts.

(NICHOLAS approaches the table and opens the book.)

RACHEL: I shuffle through the listings. I look under the letter B. I find my name. My phone number. Strange? Perhaps. But not enough to hang a man. *(Pause)* And then suddenly there it is. The last entry on the page. Barnes. R Barnes. And under this name, two words: No listing.

(A beam of light cuts across the stage.)

RACHEL: Suddenly a light's turned on in the next room. I hear movement. I duck behind a table. I turn off the flashlight.

(NICHOLAS does this.)

RACHEL: And I wait. *(Pause)* Silence. Nothing. Then I hear a door open.

(SEITZ enters. He is wearing a dressing gown. We cannot see his face. We can only see his silhouette as he stands on the outer edge of the stage. He is motionless.)

RACHEL: He's in the room. I know this. I feel his presence. Does he know I'm here? What I'm looking for? Maybe not. Maybe I've outwitted him. I wait. I can almost hear him thinking.

(SEITZ turns and exits.)

RACHEL: Then he walks out.

(The beam of light is shut off.)

RACHEL: I stand. I stumble forward, grabbing the book as I go. *(He does.)* I'm out the window.

(NICHOLAS *climbs through the window frame.*)

RACHEL: Down the lawn and into the night. I have it. I have my proof.

(NICHOLAS *comes around from the exterior of the window and moves to the center of the stage.*)

RACHEL: R Barnes. The name of a woman he has no business knowing. R Barnes. The confirmation that I am not losing my mind. I stay awake. I stay alert. And when the Bethesda Oil Building opens the next morning, I'm standing in the lobby.

Scene 16

(SEITZ *enters. He sees* NICHOLAS *and stops. A moment. We are in the outer lobby of the Bethesda Oil Building.*)

SEITZ: Nicholas. I wasn't expecting to see you. Do we have a meeting scheduled for today? *(Pause)* Nicholas?

NICHOLAS: I know.

SEITZ: You...know?

NICHOLAS: What's going on. *(He begins to advance on* SEITZ.) Behind everything. You. The money out of my account. You. The bad checks. The files.

SEITZ: I—

NICHOLAS: Deleting my research. My life! You!

(NICHOLAS *hits* SEITZ *in the chest with both of his hands.*)

SEITZ: What in the world—?

(NICHOLAS *grabs* SEITZ *and throws him to the ground.*)

NICHOLAS: The beggar in the street! YOU! *(He kicks him.)* The box in my apartment! YOU! *(He kicks him again.)* The calls at three A M! YOU! YOU! *(And again)* WHAT THE HELL HAVE YOU DONE WITH MY COUSIN, YOU SON OF A BITCH?

SEITZ: Your…cousin?

NICHOLAS: YOU WORM! YOU BASTARD! YOU
MISERABLE SHIT! *(He continues to kick him.)* GET UP
SO I CAN KILL YOU!

SEITZ: I—

NICHOLAS: Where is she?

SEITZ: Who?

NICHOLAS: R Barnes! R Barnes! Her name's in your
fucking phone book! *(He pulls the book out of his pocket
and throws it at* SEITZ *on the floor.)* She came here. Told
me about you. What you were trying to do to her.

SEITZ: I don't—

NICHOLAS: Then she disappeared and everything went
bad.

SEITZ: Don't…know who—

*(*NICHOLAS *leans down and pulls* SEITZ *up off the floor by
the lapels.)*

NICHOLAS: WHERE IS SHE?

SEITZ: Nicholas…Reginald Barnes is my internal
auditor.

(Silence. This stops NICHOLAS *cold.)*

NICHOLAS: You…? *(Pause)* You're making this up.

SEITZ: It's the truth. I don't know this woman. Please.
I'm begging you. Don't kick me anymore.

*(*SEITZ *begins to cough. He spits up some blood.* NICHOLAS
lowers him to the ground.)

NICHOLAS: Oh, God. *(He begins to back away.)* Oh,
Christ.

(Then he turns and runs off. SEITZ *attempts to stand.
Slowly, painfully, he pulls himself up and stumbles offstage.)*

Scene 17

(For a moment the stage is empty. Then we hear the sound of someone knocking. Again. MARTIN *enters. He is naked except for a pair of boxer shorts. We are in his apartment. He crosses the stage and exits. A second later he reappears with* NICHOLAS.*)*

NICHOLAS: I'm sorry to bother you, but—

MARTIN: What time is it?

NICHOLAS: I didn't know—

MARTIN: What are you doing here?

NICHOLAS: I had nowhere else to go.

MARTIN: Well, you can't stay here. Nick, listen to me. This is not the place.

NICHOLAS: I'm going to be disbarred.

MARTIN: Disbarred? Are you nuts? There's an army of police after your ass!

NICHOLAS: I know. Cops. Outside my condo. And my stuff! My furniture!

MARTIN: Your what?

NICHOLAS: They threw it out! Evicted me! Took my car! Repossessed it! I have no place to live!

MARTIN: Yeah, well, that'll happen if you piss all over your loans.

NICHOLAS: They're after me!

MARTIN: Of course, they're after you, you idiot. You attacked a client. A man in a position to hurt you bad.

NICHOLAS: I fucked up.

MARTIN: Fucked up? Are you kidding me? You are the poster child for the word catastrophe.

NICHOLAS: I know, I know, I…need to borrow some money.

MARTIN: I'm sorry?

NICHOLAS: You said you'd loan me—

MARTIN: Yeah, I know, but that was before you became Joe Psycho.

NICHOLAS: Martin—

MARTIN: The answer is no, okay? Now, please, let's not make this any nastier than it has to be.

(From offstage we hear a voice.)

LOUISE: Who is that? *(She enters. She is naked except for a sheet that she has wrapped around herself. She sees* NICHOLAS *and stops.)* Oh, uh…hi, Nick. We, um…saw you on the news.

*(*NICHOLAS *opens his mouth to speak, but no words come out.)*

MARTIN: Let me handle this, okay? Please. Go back to bed.

*(*LOUISE *looks at* NICHOLAS. *Then she turns and exits. A moment.)*

NICHOLAS: You and she—?

MARTIN: Look, I'm sorry about this. I empathize with your situation. Whatever that means. But right now you have to get out of my apartment. Otherwise I'm going to call the authorities.

NICHOLAS: You can't—

MARTIN: No. I'm going to call them anyway. But I still want you gone.

NICHOLAS: You've got to help me.

MARTIN: Actually, that is *not* something I have to do.

NICHOLAS: Please!

MARTIN: Listen. Buddy. Out. The night is young. Go find yourself a park bench to crap on. Better yet, turn yourself in.

NICHOLAS: I HAVE NOWHERE TO GO!

MARTIN: We all have our problems. But truthfully, Nicholas, do you think I give a shit? You're dreaming. Now farewell. Adios. Don't loiter in my hallway. And don't stand anywhere near my life. Alright? Thank you. Goodnight. (*He exits.*)

Scene 18

(RACHEL *enters with the journal.* NICHOLAS *picks up a whiskey bottle and moves to the center of the stage.*)

RACHEL: I return to the streets. The blanket of the night. So long as I stay moving, I think, so long as I'm in motion I'm somehow safe. I walk under freeways. Down avenues. Spend my last few dollars on a bottle of bad liquor. I don't stop. I don't look back.

(*We hear the sounds of water and sea gulls and a boat blowing a horn in the distance.*)

RACHEL: It's after midnight. I find myself on the end of a long pier looking out over the ocean. I take a drink.

(NICHOLAS *does.*)

RACHEL: I see everything now. From this perspective. The pier. Being on the edge of the pier gives me something. Distance. A sense of isolation. I take another drink.

(NICHOLAS *does.*)

RACHEL: How could I have been so wrong? I wanted, needed a scapegoat. Someone to blame for these inexplicable events. This turn. This total abandonment. I look at my watch.

(NICHOLAS *does.*)

RACHEL: Two minutes past three o'clock. When everything you believe is held up to question. When there are no absolute truths and all the world is suspect.

(NICHOLAS *drinks.*)

RACHEL: The bottle is empty. I want to let it go. I want to let go. I'm drawn down into the water below. A promise of sleep. An end to this pain. I look up.

(NICHOLAS *does.*)

RACHEL: Suddenly I feel a surge of energy. And then I'm falling through the air.

(There is a flash of light. AMELIA *enters. She slowly crosses the stage and sings.)*

AMELIA: In the winter night when the earth is white, We will lay our bodies down

(The DERELICT *enters at the rear of the stage and slowly crosses.)*

AMELIA: And those things we feel and hold as real Will drift away and drown.

*(*LOUISE *and* MARTIN *enter. They are fully clothed now. He carefully lays an old mattress on the center of the stage. She throws a sheet across the mattress.* SEITZ *enters from another direction and slowly crosses.)*

AMELIA:
Through the darkened world, we will fall unfurled To the finish of our days.

*(*NICHOLAS *moves to the mattress. He lies down on it.* LOUISE *and* MARTIN *take the bottle from* NICHOLAS. *They take his tie. They remove his shoes and the watch from his hand.)*

AMELIA: In the reeling black, we'll then reach back
To the marigolds and maize,

(LOUISE *and* MARTIN *exit.* SEITZ *looks down at* NICHOLAS *and exits. The* DERELICT *completes his cross, looks at* NICHOLAS, *and exits.*)

AMELIA: To the marigolds and maize.

(AMELIA *exits.* RACHEL *returns the journal to her pocket. She crosses to the bed and looks down at* NICHOLAS. *His eyes are closed.*)

RACHEL: Nicholas?

(*There is no response.* RACHEL *leans down. She touches* NICHOLAS, *gently.*)

RACHEL: Nicholas?

(NICHOLAS *opens his eyes. He looks at* RACHEL. *A moment.*)

NICHOLAS: Are you the doctor?

RACHEL: No.

(*Pause*)

NICHOLAS: You're not the doctor?

RACHEL: No.

(*Pause*)

NICHOLAS: What are you?

RACHEL: I'm your cousin.

END OF ACT ONE

ACT TWO

Scene 1

(NICHOLAS *lies on the mattress.* RACHEL *stands beside him. We are in a hotel for transients. No time has passed from the end of the previous scene.*)

NICHOLAS: Where's the doctor?

RACHEL: There is no doctor. You're in a hotel, Nicholas. For transients. They took your watch. Your shoes. They let you stay here.

NICHOLAS: Rachel?

(RACHEL *nods.*)

NICHOLAS: They took my shoes?

RACHEL: Yeah.

(NICHOLAS *sits up and looks at his feet.*)

NICHOLAS: Those were my good shoes. *(Pause)* How's your brother? *(Pause)* Your brother's dead.

RACHEL: That's right.

NICHOLAS: I should be dead.

RACHEL: What happened?

NICHOLAS: I don't know. *(Pause)* I hit the water and went down. Couldn't breathe. Couldn't feel anything. I was fading. Then…something happened.

RACHEL: What?

NICHOLAS: I wanted to live. *(Pause)* I came up and grabbed hold of a chain. I hung on till I got my strength back. Then I swam to shore. Got out. Went looking for a place. A room. A hotel. *(Pause)* This hotel.

RACHEL: Yeah.

NICHOLAS: How long have I been here?

RACHEL: Almost a week.

NICHOLAS: A week. *(Pause)* Where did you go?

RACHEL: How do you mean?

NICHOLAS: You disappeared. I tried to find you. Tried to call.

RACHEL: The phone was disconnected. The locks were changed. I couldn't get into my loft.

NICHOLAS: Why?

RACHEL: Because I couldn't pay the bills. I didn't have any money. It had all been…taken away. People I thought I knew they…became something else. There were these calls. Messages.

NICHOLAS: From her.

RACHEL: Yeah.

NICHOLAS: Amelia.

RACHEL: Yeah. *(Pause)* One night I came home and found the front door open. The loft was empty. But in the middle of the room there was a set of combs with silver handles. They used to belong to Grandma. They were hers.

NICHOLAS: Was there ever a man?

RACHEL: A man?

NICHOLAS: A derelict. In the street. Looking up.

RACHEL: Yes. I saw him. And before. He came to me. He said I'd be—

NICHOLAS: Next in line.

RACHEL: Next in line. *(Pause)* Then I was thrown out of the building. Didn't know where to go. I started walking. Then I ran. Then I got a ride in a truck.

NICHOLAS: You came here.

RACHEL: I heard the police were after you. It was in the papers. But there was another story, too. *(She pulls a piece of newsprint out of her pocket and hands it to him.)* This item about a man who fell off the Santa Monica Pier. A couple on the beach saw you. Said you pulled yourself out. I came here and found those people. They told me the last thing they saw was you wandering down the boardwalk. Toward this building.

NICHOLAS: Rachel, how did your parents die?

(RACHEL moves away and lights up a cigarette.)

RACHEL: In a car accident.

NICHOLAS: How?

RACHEL: Coming home from a trip. They'd driven down to Portland for a few days to see someone. An old friend from college. I think they asked him for a loan. And I think he said no. And on the way back… the car went off the side of a cliff.

NICHOLAS: Was it an accident?

RACHEL: That's what everybody told me.

NICHOLAS: And did you believe them?

(Pause)

RACHEL: No.

NICHOLAS: My father took his own life. And so did my mom.

RACHEL: My God.

NICHOLAS: And I—

RACHEL: You almost did the same thing.

NICHOLAS: Yeah. *(Pause)* This is all that's left now, Rachel. You. And me.

RACHEL: Yeah, I figured that out. *(Pause)* We have to get you out of here.

NICHOLAS: Okay.

RACHEL: Cleaned up.

NICHOLAS: Okay.

RACHEL: And then we have to go.

NICHOLAS: Where?

RACHEL: You know where.

(Pause)

NICHOLAS: The farm.

RACHEL: Yeah.

NICHOLAS: Grandma's farm.

RACHEL: We're going to Pennsylvania.

NICHOLAS: With what?

(RACHEL *pulls out a small collection of bills.)*

RACHEL: I still have some cash they didn't get.

NICHOLAS: They?

RACHEL: Yeah.

NICHOLAS: Who?

RACHEL: I don't know!

NICHOLAS: No, I can't.

RACHEL: What?

NICHOLAS: Can't do it.

RACHEL: You *can* and you're *going* to.

NICHOLAS: But why?

RACHEL: Why? *(She laughs.)* I thought that you were smart. That they were going to make you a partner. An associate.

NICHOLAS: They were.

RACHEL: Then *be* smart and put it together. It's the one place that everything points to. Everything that's happened. To you. To me. To my brother. *That's* where it leads. Where it *connects.* And if you can't see that, can't make sense of that, then I feel sorry for you. But I'm not going to stay. I'm going to leave you right here in this hotel and you deserve whatever happens. *(She starts to go.)*

NICHOLAS: Alright. I'll go. I'll go with you.

RACHEL: Good.

(NICHOLAS stands up.)

NICHOLAS: Rachel?

RACHEL: What?

(He looks at his feet. He looks at her. A moment.)

NICHOLAS: Where are my shoes?

Scene 2

(RACHEL reaches into one of the boxes and pulls out a pair of shoes. She hands them to NICHOLAS who puts them on. LOUISE and MARTIN enter. They remove the sheet, restore the mattress, and exit. GEDDES walks on. He joins NICHOLAS and RACHEL. They look out over the audience. The lighting shifts. The stage seems to open up. We are in another part of the world. The top of a hill in Evansville, Pennsylvania. A cemetery. It is early morning. We hear the sound of birds chirping. GEDDES carries a thermos and sips coffee from a cup.)

GEDDES: Beautiful country. You feel it in your hands. On your face. In the light across the fields. This time of day is unique. Just before the sun comes up. All is promise. Promise and pardon. The new world. You look out there and you see what they meant. Long time ago.

RACHEL: Yeah.

GEDDES: How long you been traveling?

RACHEL: Four, five days. We took a bus from Los Angeles.

GEDDES: Plane would have been faster.

RACHEL: It was all we could afford.

GEDDES: Let's see now. You I don't recall. What did you say your name was?

RACHEL: Rachel Barnes.

GEDDES: Uh-huh. You Wyatt's girl?

RACHEL: That's right.

GEDDES: He your brother?

RACHEL: No. My cousin. Nicholas.

GEDDES: Nicholas. *(He looks at* NICHOLAS.*)* Oh, sure. Same features as your father. Benjamin Barnes.

NICHOLAS: That's right.

GEDDES: Sure. I remember you as a boy. Used to...I'm trying to recall now. There's a picture in my head. You had an airplane.

NICHOLAS: No.

GEDDES: A piece of wood. Tied onto a string. Used to drag it around like it was your airplane.

NICHOLAS: I...that's true. I did. *(Pause)* What's your name?

GEDDES: Don't matter. *(Pause. He sips from his cup.)*
Geddes.

RACHEL: Do you live in Evansville, Mr Geddes?

GEDDES: All my life. Thus far. I own the parts store you
saw coming into town.

NICHOLAS: Oh.

GEDDES: You didn't see it?

NICHOLAS: No, I did.

GEDDES: You're a liar. But that's alright. I got a hole in
my head when it comes to the Barnes family.

NICHOLAS: Really?

RACHEL: Why is that, Mr Geddes?

(Pause. GEDDES sips.)

GEDDES: Yes, sir. Beautiful time of day.

RACHEL: It is.

GEDDES: I saw you two before. Standing down there at
the bottom of the hill. Looking up. Saw you climb this
way and walk into the cemetery. Nice up here, huh?

NICHOLAS: Yeah.

GEDDES: Peaceful. All these headstones. History.
Look here. *(He points to a space in the ground.)* Michael
Squires. You know who he was?

NICHOLAS: No.

GEDDES: Ship's carpenter. Came over in Eighteen
Seventeen. Met a lady in Philadelphia. Fell in love. And
started up a farm. Had seven children. The eldest boy
was named Wilson. He's buried right there. *(He points.)*
Took over the farm after his father died. Four children.
Three girls. And a boy named Andrew. Right there.
(He points.) Now Andrew gets the farm. Marries an

older woman who dies in childbirth. But her daughter survives.

NICHOLAS: Amelia. Amelia Squires.

(GEDDES *looks at* NICHOLAS.)

GEDDES: You know the end of this story?

NICHOLAS: No.

GEDDES: You want me to tell it?

NICHOLAS: Certainly.

(Pause)

GEDDES: Andrew and his daughter stay on the farm, but he needs help. Drifter comes to town. A con man named Franklin Barnes. Andrew hires him on and gives him charge of the place. And Franklin ingratiates himself. He likes Amelia, see. Wants her to be his wife. Well, anybody would. She was beautiful. Inner beauty. And out. She was sweetness itself. And when she opened her mouth. To speak. Or sing. It was like honey.

NICHOLAS: Sing?

GEDDES: Oh, yeah. Sounded like an angel. A heavenly angel.

NICHOLAS: She sang songs?

GEDDES: Sure. Made 'em up. Mostly. *(Pause)* You didn't know that?

NICHOLAS: No, I— *(He decides not to pursue this.)* Nothing. *(Pause)* Go on.

GEDDES: Well, Franklin proposes to her, but Amelia says no. And Andrew goes to Amelia and asks her to reconsider. For the sake of the farm. For the benefit of all concerned. She doesn't want to do it. But finally she consents. And Amelia Squires and Franklin Barnes get married in the town church. Right over there. *(He points.)* Must be sixty years ago now, but I remember it like it was last week. I was there, see. Following winter your great-grandfather dies.

RACHEL: So it was a marriage of convenience. Is that what you're saying? Because Andrew needed someone to take over the property?

GEDDES: Some people saw it that way.

RACHEL: And Franklin Barnes was able to convince Andrew that he was the man for the job.

GEDDES: Sometimes you don't recognize what's there in front of you. Your own people. An outsider with a firm handshake and an easy manner can look mighty attractive. Especially with promises for the future. Promises of wealth. Prosperity. Things not quite possible, but nice to dream on. *(Pause)* Yes, sir. Whole history of the Squires family buried in this cemetery. Let me ask you something. You see anything up here with the name Amelia Barnes on it?

NICHOLAS: No.

GEDDES: Curious, don't you think? *(Pause)* You going by the old place?

NICHOLAS: Jesus, is…is it still there?

GEDDES: Certainly. Property don't belong to you people no more. The county claimed it. They boarded it up. Too much trouble to tear down, I suppose.

NICHOLAS: And the farm?

(GEDDES laughs.)

GEDDES: Well, you can't really call it a farm, anymore. It's all overgrown. A lot of bramble and bush. But the land's still there. Same place Michael Squires settled on almost two hundred years ago. *(Pause)* Time to get to work. *(He starts to exit.)*

NICHOLAS: Mr Geddes—

GEDDES: You come by and see me 'fore you leave town. It's the parts store on your way out. Can't miss it. *(He exits.)*

Scene 3

(NICHOLAS and RACHEL turn and take in their surroundings. The lighting shifts to reveal the room they have been occupying since the beginning of the play. We are in the attic of the house that once belonged to Amelia Barnes. NICHOLAS and RACHEL slowly move through the room, touching the remaining objects and pieces of furniture. It is afternoon.)

RACHEL: How long has it been, do you think?

NICHOLAS: Since when?

RACHEL: Since anyone's been up here?

NICHOLAS: I don't know. Ten years. Twenty.

(RACHEL turns and looks at the window.)

RACHEL: I wonder if that window still opens.

NICHOLAS: One way to find out. *(He goes to the window and opens it. He looks out.)* Well, the old man was right about one thing.

RACHEL: What's that?

NICHOLAS: It's not a farm anymore.

(RACHEL goes to the window. They stand together looking out. A moment)

RACHEL: But it used to be. There used to be something growing out there. Though even as a girl I remember thinking it's going to seed.

NICHOLAS: I guess our fathers weren't exactly cut out to be landowners, huh?

RACHEL: Uh, no, not exactly. *(She turns away from the window and moves back into the room.)* This room was like our playhouse, Nicholas. Our hideout. Do you remember that?

NICHOLAS: I do.

RACHEL: It was filled with old furniture and paintings and photographs.

NICHOLAS: And something else. Wasn't there a…?

RACHEL: A what?

NICHOLAS: A chest. A hope chest. *(He turns and sees the wooden chest and goes to it. He hesitates. Then he opens it and looks inside.)* Empty.

RACHEL: That was Grandma's. I remember her telling us about it once. How it was brought over on the boat by one of her ancestors.

NICHOLAS: Michael Squires.

RACHEL: Yeah.

NICHOLAS: Which makes it older than the house. Older than the farm. *(Pause)* I remember going through it as a kid. Unwrapping things. Antiques. Artifacts. *(Pause)* Oh, my God.

RACHEL: What?

NICHOLAS: Her music box. This is where I first saw it. This is where it was kept. Inside this chest. And something else. *(Pause)* Her combs. The ones with the silver handles. This is where they came from. *(Pause)* Somebody remembered that, Rachel. Somebody besides us.

RACHEL: *You* remembered.

NICHOLAS: What?

RACHEL: About the chest—

NICHOLAS: Well, I— *(Pause)* Have no explanation.

RACHEL: No?

NICHOLAS: No. It simply…stuck in my head. *(Pause)* What are you thinking?

RACHEL: Nothing.

NICHOLAS: Why are you looking at me that way?

RACHEL: No reason.

NICHOLAS: You think I might be a part of it.

RACHEL: No.

NICHOLAS: A part of their scheme. Their machinations. Whoever it is that's doing this. You think I'm one of them. That I'm out to get you.

RACHEL: Well, I mean, my God, Nicholas, everything's been a blur to you. Your life. Your childhood. And then *that*. You remember *that*.

NICHOLAS: I told you—

RACHEL: Close the window.

NICHOLAS: What?

RACHEL: Close it.

NICHOLAS: Why?

RACHEL: Because I'm cold.

(NICHOLAS does.)

RACHEL: I mean, hadn't you ever wondered about *me*? When I came to you? When I tried to tell you what was going on? Didn't it occur to you? Maybe *she's* in on it, too?

NICHOLAS: Not till this moment. *(Pause)* Are you?

RACHEL: No.

NICHOLAS: Okay. *(Pause)* Neither am I. *(Pause)* Now would be a good time to say I believe you.

RACHEL: I—

NICHOLAS: You know what? Don't. Don't say anything.

RACHEL: Nicholas—

NICHOLAS: You brought me out here. To the middle of nowhere. Some miserable shack that's about to collapse. To accuse me? Come at me?

RACHEL: No!

NICHOLAS: I don't need any of this.

(NICHOLAS *starts to go.*)

RACHEL: I believe you!

(NICHOLAS *stops.*)

RACHEL: I do. (*Awkwardly, she extends a hand.*) Please.

(NICHOLAS *looks at* RACHEL. *Then he comes forward. She reaches out and embraces him. He holds her. He starts to shake. To cry. She holds onto him.* AMELIA *enters. She slowly moves through the room and sings.*)

AMELIA: In the summer light when the fields are bright
And the sky is full of praise,
We will fill our cup and lift it up
To the starting of our days.

We will make our schemes, we will dream our dreams
With no why or where or when,
But that fragrant wine that was so fine
Will never come again.

Scene 4

(GEDDES *enters as* AMELIA *exits. He carries a soup bowl with a spoon in it.* RACHEL *goes to him and he hands her the bowl. She drinks from it.* NICHOLAS *sits. We are on the back porch of* GEDDES's *parts store. It is evening and we hear the sound of crickets.*)

GEDDES: Your grandfather, Franklin Barnes, was a
weak man. Unfit to run a farm. Everything went bad
under his spell. Property suffered. Amelia got sick.
Had three children and the last one almost killed her.
Then one day she wakes up and Franklin has headed
out for parts unknown. Rumor has it he hit the road
with a prostitute from Fredericksburg. That's the
fiction, anyway. What your grandma used to call true
fiction. You finished with that soup?

RACHEL: Yeah.

GEDDES: Give me the bowl.

(RACHEL *does.*)

GEDDES: How about you, son? You sure you're not
hungry?

NICHOLAS: No.

GEDDES: How about a beer?

NICHOLAS: Where's our grandmother buried?

(*A moment.* GEDDES *leans down and pantomimes picking
up a small stone, which he tosses over the heads of the
audience. He watches it go.*)

GEDDES: A stone drops in the water. It makes this
ripple for a while and then it goes away. We can't see it
no more. We think it's gone. But it's out there. Moving.
Somewhere. Same thing between people. Now I touch
you. (*He looks at* NICHOLAS.) And you remember that.

NICHOLAS: I will. Whatever you tell me. I promise. I'll
remember.

(*Pause*)

GEDDES: After Franklin left town, Amelia tried to run
the farm alone. Not enough money in the till to hire on
much help and the boys, Benjamin, Wyatt, well, they're
practically useless. So everyday she's out there in the
fields trying to make something out of this property

of hers. Boys grow up. Go to college. Get themselves
jobs in the professional world and move away. But the
daughter, Jacqueline, she stays behind with her mother
and has a child out of wedlock. What they used to call
a love child.

RACHEL: Eugene.

NICHOLAS: Cousin Eugene.

GEDDES: That's right. *(Pause)* Now every so often the
boys come back home with their pretty, little wives and
well-mannered children. But every time they do there's
fireworks. Boys want Amelia to sell the property and
make themselves a profit. There's been offers, see, and
those two can almost taste that money. But Amelia
says no. It's all she has. Boys go away, but they're still
scheming. *(Pause)* One morning, Amelia's out on the
fields and takes a fall. Twists her ankle. Has to be laid
up in the hospital for a few weeks. Well, the boys drive
into town, dump some flowers on her bed, and find a
doctor. And they ask that man to declare their mother
incompetent.

NICHOLAS: What?

GEDDES: Incompetent. Mentally unstable. Unable to
take care of herself and think clearly. The daughter,
Jacqueline, she fights them, of course, but she's only
one against two. Within a week the legal work is
done and the boys have sold off the farm, the house,
and most of the furniture. Amelia comes out of that
hospital all healed up with no home to return to. Boys
have her set up in one of those institutions for people
whose family no longer has a place for them. She
curses her two children. She cries out and complains,
but there's nothing to be done. In the end she goes.
And three days later she dies.

NICHOLAS: In the institution?

GEDDES: So far as I know.

NICHOLAS: Alone?

GEDDES: Yes, sir. *(Pause)* Not exactly the family portrait you wanted to pull out of the archives, huh?

NICHOLAS: No.

GEDDES: Well, there it lies.

RACHEL: They had no right.

GEDDES: No, ma'am.

RACHEL: No right to do what they did.

GEDDES: Nevertheless, that's what happened.

NICHOLAS: That still doesn't tell me—

GEDDES: Where she's buried. The truth is I don't know. I wasn't at the funeral, see. It was a private affair. Just family.

RACHEL: Aunt Jacqueline?

GEDDES: Yeah?

RACHEL: What ever happened to her?

GEDDES: They said her heart was broke in half when your grandma died. She left town. Took her child and went away.

NICHOLAS: She did?

GEDDES: Got married.

NICHOLAS: Really?

GEDDES: So I'm told. Fella from out west. Hank or Henry or something. An oil man.

(Pause)

NICHOLAS: An...an oil man?

GEDDES: So I heard.

NICHOLAS: Harry? Harrison?

GEDDES: Could be.

NICHOLAS: Harrison Seitz?

GEDDES: Seitz. That sounds about right. See, I'd almost forgot. *(He looks at* NICHOLAS.*)* But you won't now, will you? *(Pause)* Turn out the porch light before you go. *(He starts to exit.)*

RACHEL: Mr Geddes?

GEDDES: One more question and then I got to get what little sleep I can.

RACHEL: My grandmother—

GEDDES: Yes?

RACHEL: Amelia Squires—

GEDDES: Go on.

RACHEL: Were you ever in love with her?

(Pause)

GEDDES: I was *always* in love with her. Grade school. High school. People used to say we made the perfect couple. That it was predetermined. But life transpires. Sometimes it goes in your favor. And sometimes it grinds against you. And everything fades, young lady. That's no fiction. *(He exits. A moment)*

NICHOLAS: Seitz.

RACHEL: Who?

NICHOLAS: The man I told you about. The one I attacked. Thinking he was behind it all. Christ, Rachel, he *was* behind it all. That means…that means she must be there somewhere close to him.

RACHEL: She?

NICHOLAS: Aunt Jacqueline. They're in it together. We'll find her. We'll go through him. We'll get to her.

RACHEL: Where?

NICHOLAS: California. L A. We'll catch the next bus.

RACHEL: I'm staying here.

(Pause)

NICHOLAS: Here?

RACHEL: I'm staying.

NICHOLAS: Why?

RACHEL: To live. To work. I'll do...something. Anything. To earn the money.

NICHOLAS: For what?

RACHEL: The house. I want to buy back the house. *(Pause)* I want to live here.

NICHOLAS: You're not serious.

RACHEL: I am.

NICHOLAS: Rachel, it's a deathtrap. A wreck.

RACHEL: I'll fix it up.

NICHOLAS: We don't have the money.

RACHEL: I'll *earn* the money. I just *said* that. It's what I'm going to *do*.

NICHOLAS: But—

RACHEL: Listen. I heard it. This afternoon. When we were alone in the house. The attic.

(Pause)

NICHOLAS: What?

RACHEL: That song. It's her. I know it. Like she's trying to reach out to me from the other side. Trying to tell me something.

NICHOLAS: Grandma.

RACHEL: Yes. *(Pause)* You've heard it, too.

NICHOLAS: Sometimes, I…think I hear…something. I don't know. She sounds so young.

RACHEL: She *was* young, once. She was alive.

NICHOLAS: But it doesn't make any sense.

RACHEL: Why does it have to make sense?

NICHOLAS: It's one of their tricks.

RACHEL: No.

NICHOLAS: Their treacheries.

RACHEL: Nicholas—

NICHOLAS: I don't know how they did it. But I'm going to figure it out. I swear to you. I'm going to go there. Find them. Face them straight on.

RACHEL: Why?

NICHOLAS: Why? *(He laughs.)* Don't you want justice? For your mom and dad? Your brother? Yourself?

RACHEL: Maybe they were right.

NICHOLAS: What?

RACHEL: Maybe they were right to do what they did. *(Pause)* Maybe we deserved it.

NICHOLAS: Deserved it? *(He laughs again.)* Well, I don't know about you, Rachel, but, no. No, I do not deserve this. This has nothing to do with me.

RACHEL: How can you be so sure?

NICHOLAS: Because I am! Because my life has been blown apart! Decimated! I have to find those people responsible. I have to set things right. *(Pause)* You could come with me.

RACHEL: You could stay here.

NICHOLAS: No. I can't. I'm sorry.

RACHEL: Me, too.

(A moment. NICHOLAS *and* RACHEL *stand looking at each other. Not moving)*

RACHEL: We could have turned it all around.

NICHOLAS: What do you mean?

RACHEL: The house. The farm. *(Pause)* Stay in touch.

*(*RACHEL *touches* NICHOLAS *lightly, then exits. He watches her go. He stands alone.)*

Scene 5

*(*SEITZ *and* MARTIN *enter together.* NICHOLAS *turns to them. We are in the outer lobby of the Bethesda Oil Building.)*

SEITZ: Mr Barnes. What a painful surprise to have you back with us at Bethesda Oil. Call the police, Martin.

MARTIN: Yes, sir. *(He exits.)*

SEITZ: Now. You have less than seven minutes before they arrive. I'd be curious to learn what it is you hope to accomplish in that time. From a distance.

NICHOLAS: I know who J B is.

SEITZ: J B?

NICHOLAS: The ex-wife whose portfolio you look after. J B. Jacqueline Barnes. My aunt.

SEITZ: Is this someone I should know, Nicholas? Someone bordering on schizophrenia like yourself?

NICHOLAS: Maybe. *(Pause)* You've just divorced your third wife. Number two was an airline stewardess you met flying over Singapore. But your first wife, who's listed everywhere I've looked as J B Seitz, was, in fact, Jacqueline Barnes. Which makes you, at some point in time, my uncle. What a disgusting thought.

SEITZ: Six minutes.

NICHOLAS: She must have something on you. Observations from all those years of watching you maneuver and manipulate. So here's the deal, she says. I've got this familial vendetta I want to play out. And you're going to help me. *(Pause)* Where is she? Where do I find Jacqueline Barnes?

SEITZ: I have no idea. *(He starts to go.)*

NICHOLAS: I'll prove that you were behind it.

SEITZ: No. *(Pause)* No, that you will never do. That simply cannot be accomplished.

(MARTIN enters.)

MARTIN: They're on their way.

SEITZ: Good. Stay with him till they arrive.

(SEITZ exits. MARTIN turns and looks at NICHOLAS.)

MARTIN: Listen—

NICHOLAS: How's the new position working out, old buddy? Quite a promotion over your previous gig. You must be giddy with excitement.

MARTIN: I want to explain—

NICHOLAS: And the getting here was so easy. All you had to do was hang around my office long enough to learn my password, access my computer, and dump my research. Or did you simply let him into the building and he took care of the rest?

MARTIN: I never—

NICHOLAS: Now, what I question the wisdom of, old buddy, old sport, was the brief liaison with Louise. I say brief knowing that your commitment to any one woman lasts about twenty minutes. Was that extracurricular? Something you concocted with your own feeble manhood? Or was she in on it, too?

MARTIN: Look—

NICHOLAS: Jesus, she was. Of course, she was. Tell her I want to see her. *(He starts to exit.)*

MARTIN: Hey!

(NICHOLAS turns on MARTIN.)

NICHOLAS: You're going to stop me from leaving, old buddy, old sport, old pal?

(NICHOLAS backhands MARTIN across the face. Then he punches him in the stomach. MARTIN collapses to the ground.)

NICHOLAS: You forget, I'm a violent man.

(He pulls MARTIN up by the hair and he cries out.)

MARTIN: Ah!

NICHOLAS: You tell Louise I want to talk to her. Otherwise word gets back to your new boss that all this conjecture came right out of your mouth. Got it?

MARTIN: Uh-huh.

NICHOLAS: Beautiful. I'll be in the park. By my old building.

(NICHOLAS drops MARTIN to the floor and exits.)

Scene 6

(LOUISE enters. She sits. MARTIN stands, brushes the dirt from his trousers, and exits. A moment. NICHOLAS enters. He is wearing the weather-beaten overcoat, torn sweater, and pants that we first saw him in. He sees her. He smiles. He sits down beside her. We are in a public park. We hear the sounds of children laughing and distant traffic. For a moment, neither of them speak.)

NICHOLAS: Nice to see you. *(Pause)* To be seen with you, I mean. Here among the pigeons. You fit right in.

LOUISE: I—

NICHOLAS: See how they coo and strut? These fat birds? Bloated. Insatiable. Sick with disease.

LOUISE: Look—

NICHOLAS: You could form a club.

(LOUISE starts to go and NICHOLAS grabs onto her.)

NICHOLAS: Sorry. I wasn't going to start this way. Let's talk about something else. *(Pause)* This a new outfit, no? A new look for you?

LOUISE: Yes.

NICHOLAS: I like it. It reeks of money. Ripped right out of my wallet.

LOUISE: I never—

NICHOLAS: There I go again. Bringing up the buried past. Christ, that was what? Two, three months ago? You'd think I would have forgotten by now.

LOUISE: I was told—

NICHOLAS: I've been trying to figure out what the deal was. Here's what I've surmised. You provide them with my info, my I D, the numbers in my accounts, and they pay you back with a percentage of the proceeds. They don't need the money. The effect is simply to wipe me out.

LOUISE: I was told—

NICHOLAS: Yes?

LOUISE: That you wanted to see me.

(Pause)

NICHOLAS: I'm looking for my aunt.

LOUISE: I don't know where she is.

(Pause. NICHOLAS reaches into the pocket of his overcoat and produces the photograph of his family.)

NICHOLAS: I've been carrying this thing around with me. This photograph that Rachel gave me that night at the airport. I remember you saying I had big ears as a kid. I also remember you pointing to my aunt. Out of all the women in this picture. You picked her out. Someone who I'd never mentioned before or since. *(Pause)* Where is she?

LOUISE: Why don't you go away, Nick?

NICHOLAS: You could give me a tip, here. No one would have to know. It would be our little secret.

LOUISE: You really should leave town. I...I could lend you some money.

(LOUISE *holds out a wad of bills.* NICHOLAS *looks at it. He laughs.)*

NICHOLAS: You're going to lend me my own money? That's rich, Louise.

LOUISE: I can't help.

NICHOLAS: You owe me.

LOUISE: No.

NICHOLAS: Yes. They used you. In an attempt to break me. I want to find that woman. I want to know where she is.

LOUISE: Why?

NICHOLAS: I would think that would be obvious. I want see to them laid out. Cut open. Ripped in two.

LOUISE: Well, good luck, Nick. I've got my personal safety to think about. *(She stands.)* Can I offer you some advice?

NICHOLAS: No.

LOUISE: You can listen anyway. What happened to you was bad. I...have some regrets about what I did. Some. Not enough to put myself at risk, but enough to feel some sense of... *(She doesn't know what to call it.)* Well, it was wrong, okay? I'm sorry. If you go now, I don't think they'll follow you. I think they'll let you be. But you have to go *now*.

NICHOLAS: Not a chance. I want to be there when the knife goes in. I want to *hold* that knife.

LOUISE: Well. That's too bad. Goodbye, Nicholas. *(She exits.)*

Scene 7

(NICHOLAS moves to another position. The lights dim around him. He reaches into his pocket and pulls out a piece of paper and a pencil. For a moment he writes. Then he reads aloud. We are still in the public park.)

NICHOLAS: Dear Rachel. I'm writing to you from a park bench in the old neighborhood where I used to live. It's a cool day in late November. I watch the couples come and go. Some hold hands. Some carry small children. The illusion of well-being is strong here. My life is a testament to that. I have mixed results to report to you regarding my course of action. The fact is I'm no closer to finding Jacqueline Barnes today than the night I fell into the ocean. I'm not sure how to continue. I know they're watching me. That my condition is being monitored. And that no one is to be trusted. It's the one thing that keeps me from taking a room somewhere. That and the fact that I have no money. But here's the thing. I don't mind. I've passed the point of caring. And with that comes a certain freedom. I haven't eaten in almost a week. My body is beginning to stink. I'm separated from everything I see. And it doesn't matter. I know what I want. Revenge. Nicholas. *(He signs his name, licks the envelope, and seals the letter, which he puts back in his pocket.)*

Scene 8

(NICHOLAS *moves to another position and the lights brighten around him.* SEITZ *enters eating a huge hot dog on a large bun with all the fixings. We are still in the public park.*)

NICHOLAS: Yeah?

SEITZ: Well, I had an hour to kill between appointments, so I thought I'd take a stroll through the park.

NICHOLAS: Uh-huh.

SEITZ: And see how you're bearing up.

NICHOLAS: Hey, I'm terrific. Really. Never been better.

(SEITZ *eats. He smiles at* NICHOLAS. NICHOLAS *looks away.*)

NICHOLAS: See them? The couple across the street? With the little girl?

SEITZ: Yes.

NICHOLAS: Yesterday the father told me to get out of his park. His neighborhood. He called me a fucking bum.

SEITZ: Have you seen yourself lately, Nicholas? The description is apt. You're disgusting.

NICHOLAS: Thank you.

SEITZ: And you smell badly.

NICHOLAS: So I'm told.

SEITZ: Some of your neighbors have filed a complaint.

NICHOLAS: I haven't done anything.

SEITZ: Your presence upsets them.

NICHOLAS: So what?

SEITZ: The local shelter has offered a room. A bed has been prepared.

NICHOLAS: I don't want it.

SEITZ: What do you want?

NICHOLAS: Your head. On a platter. A pear stuck up your mouth. Your entrails held out for public display. The names of your children spoken as a curse.

SEITZ: Why not just ruin my credit rating?

NICHOLAS: That, too.

SEITZ: And this is what sustains you? A dream of blood and destruction?

NICHOLAS: You got it.

SEITZ: You're worse off than you were before.

NICHOLAS: Wrong. Before I sought the accumulation of wealth. My place on the windy hill. To no specific end. Now I have a purpose.

SEITZ: And that is?

NICHOLAS: Your castration.

SEITZ: Of course.

NICHOLAS: Which is redundant.

SEITZ: How so?

NICHOLAS: Somebody already has your nuts on the table.

SEITZ: Ah.

NICHOLAS: Where is she?

(SEITZ *laughs*.)

SEITZ: Your persistence is admirable.

NICHOLAS: Is she overhead? Is she watching us?

SEITZ: But your plan of attack is positively comic. Like pissing in the wind.

NICHOLAS: Yeah, well, I've been doing a lot of that lately.

SEITZ: Another reason the neighbors complain. *(Pause)* You sent a letter to your cousin. We intercepted it. *(He pulls an envelope out of his coat that is identical to the one NICHOLAS was holding. He rips it in half. Then he lets the pieces fall to his feet.)* We know where she is. We know where *you* are, as well. The game is at an end. A bullet could pass through your head. Your body could drop into a sewer. It would not be missed. *(Pause)* You have become an embarrassment to this society, Nicholas. An outcast. A pariah with no real hope for the future. It's only a matter of days now. You will find yourself back on that pier.

NICHOLAS: No.

SEITZ: This time you won't surface.

NICHOLAS: I will.

SEITZ: The situation's clear. You're beaten.

NICHOLAS: I'm not.

SEITZ: But you are.

NICHOLAS: No.

SEITZ: It's better to state the obvious.

NICHOLAS: No.

SEITZ: Say that you're broken.

NICHOLAS: I won't.

SEITZ: Say it.

NICHOLAS: Not beaten! Or broken! Or hurting in any way! Do you understand? *You* will suffer! *You* will be brought down to your knees! But *I'm* fine! *(He shrieks.)* I'M. DOING. JUST. FINE!

(Silence)

SEITZ: I see. *(Pause)* Then I cannot help you. *(He starts to exit.)*

NICHOLAS: Don't...

SEITZ: What? *(Pause)* I'm sorry, but I can't hear you. *(Pause)* Can't make you out. *(Pause)* Speak up.

NICHOLAS: I'm lost.

SEITZ: Again.

NICHOLAS: Lost. I thought I could...dismantle your confidence. Kill the operation. Everything. I can't. I'm tired. Hungry.

SEITZ: And? *(Pause)* What else?

(Pause)

NICHOLAS: Beaten.

SEITZ: Good. *(He hands* NICHOLAS *a business card.)* Here is the address. They're ready to see you now.

Scene 9

*(*JACQUELINE *enters as* SEITZ *exits. She wears a formal gown and is somewhat unsteady on her feet. She smiles at* NICHOLAS. *He turns to her. We are in a penthouse apartment overlooking the city.)*

JACQUELINE: Well. *(Pause)* You're early. *(Pause)* That's alright, I suppose. I mean, why not? The weather's starting to turn out there. They say a cold front's coming in. So we may have a real winter here. For the holidays. The celebration. You know, New Year's Eve. The end of...well, a century of something. Surely. *(She laughs nervously.)* Did you have any trouble finding the place?

NICHOLAS: No. *(Pause)* No, the directions were very specific. *(He moves to the window.)* A penthouse apartment. Overlooking the city. With an extensive view of the skyline. The shore. *(Pause)* The pier.

JACQUELINE: Yes, we're very fortunate.

(NICHOLAS turns.)

NICHOLAS: We?

(Pause)

JACQUELINE: I fixed a meal for us. A bird, potatoes, gravy—

NICHOLAS: I'm not hungry.

JACQUELINE: But you've been without food since—

NICHOLAS: I've gotten used to it.

JACQUELINE: Yes, of course. *(Pause)* Why are you staring at me, Nicholas? Have I changed so much?

NICHOLAS: Aunt Jacqueline, you...you tried to have me killed.

JACQUELINE: No.

NICHOLAS: Tried to murder me.

JACQUELINE: I didn't do that.

NICHOLAS: You took away my life!

JACQUELINE: I took away your *assets*. Certain options. That's true. But I didn't push you out into the ocean. You did that to yourself.

NICHOLAS: I...? My God. Do you have any idea what it is that you have done?

(Then from offstage we hear another voice.)

EUGENE: Mom?

(And the DERELICT enters. He is also dressed in formal attire and carries a brown paper bag. He sees NICHOLAS and stops.)

EUGENE: Well, well. Look what the cat puked up. Hello, coz.

NICHOLAS: Eugene?

(EUGENE *smiles.*)

NICHOLAS: Cousin Eugene?

EUGENE: Good to see all that education paid off. *(He turns to* JACQUELINE.*)* You look nice, Mom.

JACQUELINE: Thanks.

EUGENE: Been drinking?

JACQUELINE: What?

EUGENE: Couldn't wait till I got back? With the booze? One night out of the year I ask you to stay relatively sober and you can't even manage *that*?

JACQUELINE: I have no idea what you—

EUGENE: Here. *(He throws her the bag.)* Have yourself a party.

(JACQUELINE *glares at* EUGENE. *Then she opens the bag and pulls out a bottle of whiskey. She finds a glass, fills it, and downs the contents.)*

EUGENE: You want anything?

NICHOLAS: No.

EUGENE: Me neither. I like to stay clear-headed. So I can concentrate. *(Pause)* So what happened? You got a little eager? A little over anxious? 'Cause I'm sure the invitation said six o'clock. But you couldn't wait, right? To see the bad girl from Pennsylvania and her bastard son? Or am I a surprise to you? Hey, I bet I am. I bet you didn't have me figured out.

NICHOLAS: No.

EUGENE: That's good. That means I'm still one step ahead of you.

NICHOLAS: I've been out east, Eugene. I've seen the farm. I know what happened.

EUGENE: Oh, yeah. Like what? What do you know, coz? I would love to hear. What the fuck did you learn?

NICHOLAS: I know that…that my father and my uncle had our grandmother declared mentally incompetent. That they sold the property. Against her wishes. And that they put her in an institution. Where she died.

EUGENE: You think she died in that place?

NICHOLAS: Yes. *(Pause)* Didn't she?

(Pause)

EUGENE: A certain someone tells me you want revenge. Is that right? You want to see us all rot in hell?

NICHOLAS: Yes.

EUGENE: Good. *(He goes to one of the tables and picks up a wooden box, which he holds out for* NICHOLAS.*)* Here.

(A moment. Then NICHOLAS *moves to* EUGENE *and takes the box.)*

EUGENE: Open it.

*(*NICHOLAS *hesitates.)*

EUGENE: Open it!

*(*NICHOLAS *does. He removes a nineteenth-century pistol from the box. He places the box on the floor and examines the gun.)*

EUGENE: That piece is ancient. From a collection that dates back to Michael Squires. Know who he is?

NICHOLAS: Yes.

EUGENE: Our great-great-great-grandfather.

NICHOLAS: I *know*.

EUGENE: Still in perfect working order.

(NICHOLAS *examines the gun.*)

NICHOLAS: It's loaded.

EUGENE: No shit.

(NICHOLAS *closes the gun.*)

NICHOLAS: Why?

EUGENE: Because I want you to understand. Why we did what we did. And then I want you to come to a decision. Hey, if I'm guilty of something, shoot me in the head. I mean it. Right here in my fancy clothes. But if I'm innocent… *(He laughs.)* Well, you'll have to figure it out. *(Pause)* You can pull the trigger anytime you want. Now. Two minutes from now. Two seconds from now. Because, like you say, your knowledge is complete. *(Pause)* No?

NICHOLAS: How did it happen?

EUGENE: How did *what* happen, coz?

NICHOLAS: How did our grandmother die?

(Pause)

EUGENE: Tell him, Mom.

JACQUELINE: Why—?

(EUGENE *shouts at* JACQUELINE.)

EUGENE: TELL HIM!

(A moment. JACQUELINE *holds her out her empty glass.* EUGENE *refills it while she talks.)*

JACQUELINE: She did go into that institution. That so-called nursing home that smelt of urine and death. And for three days she sat in a chair. Not talking. To anyone. Then in the middle of the night she found a phone and called me. She said she wanted to be taken back to the house to collect some possessions. A few personal effects. I wanted her to wait until the next morning, but she said, no, she had to go then and there and so we did. Me. My mom. And my kid.

NICHOLAS: You were there?

EUGENE: Where else would I be?

JACQUELINE: It was after midnight when we got to the house. The place was almost empty. Most of the furniture had been taken out. Sold. She sent me into the kitchen to look for her teapot. And she went up to the attic. *(Pause)* I got scared. I didn't know what we were doing there. Not really. I told Eugene to wait. Wait downstairs. And I went up. *(Pause)* I walked into the attic. And mama was kneeling in the corner of the room next to her hope chest. With a gun in her mouth. *(She points to the weapon in NICHOLAS's hand.)* That gun. *(Pause)* And then there was this sound. An explosion. And the top of her head came off.

NICHOLAS: My God.

JACQUELINE: And she's lying there. Hurt. And she won't stop. Bleeding. Her head is bleeding. Her eyes won't close. And I'm covered in blood. Her blood. It's all over me. And I'm screaming. I'm crying out because I don't know what to do. Mama. Stop bleeding. Stop the blood. Stop it. Please, please, stop. *(Silence)* And now—

EUGENE: You don't need to tell him—

JACQUELINE: Shut up! *(Pause)* Sometimes when I sleep I still see her. Or when I close my eyes in the middle of the day. She's there. The floor is red. The walls are all red. The farm's gone. Gone on and forgotten. Mama's gone, too. But I'm holding her. I'm still…holding her. *(She downs the drink.)*

EUGENE: That's the way I found them. When I came upstairs and walked into that room. Filled with blood. I'll tell you, coz, something like that stays with you.

You think, someday, somehow, people are going to be hurt. They're going to understand what it is to be thrown out of their *own* homes. To have everything *they* believe in taken away. To have nowhere to go.

(NICHOLAS *turns away from* EUGENE.)

EUGENE: But, hey, the fact that our grandmother killed herself can't be that much of a surprise.

NICHOLAS: What are you talking about?

EUGENE: You had to know.

NICHOLAS: No.

EUGENE: Oh, come on.

NICHOLAS: I was told that she died quietly in her sleep.

EUGENE: By your old man.

NICHOLAS: Yes.

EUGENE: But you knew that wasn't true.

NICHOLAS: I didn't—

EUGENE: You knew there was more to the story.

NICHOLAS: I never—

EUGENE: Asked. No. Of course not. Why would you? Hey, you couldn't even bring yourself to go to the funeral, could you? (*Pause*) Could you?

NICHOLAS: No.

EUGENE: You stayed away. You maintained this…this silence. And your family made out. My uncles could afford to send their kids to college. To law school. To medical school. To art school. But all the time you knew your success was built on a lie!

NICHOLAS: Alright, yes! (*Pause*) Yes, I knew something was wrong. Even as a boy in her house. I remember the arguments from downstairs, the fights that went on all night, the swearing and shouting coming right

up through the floorboards. I knew my father wanted
her to sell the property. And if she did our lives would
somehow be better. But she wouldn't relent. And then
with her passing there was suddenly all this *money*.
This *freedom*. We could live in a better house. My
mother could afford nicer clothes. I could go to college
and study law. So, yes. Yes, I knew these things were
somehow linked to her death. But what could I do? It
was over.

EUGENE: For you. *(Pause)* But to see what this poor lush
here—

JACQUELINE: Eugene!

EUGENE: This woman had to do to survive after we
buried Amelia two counties over in that cemetery that
allowed suicides. And my uncles wanted to give us our
share of the proceeds. And she refused. And we left
town with no resources, no plan. And the begging we
had to do to get by. The men—

JACQUELINE: Stop!

EUGENE: The sleaze, the scum buckets, the absolute
bums that came through any room we could find. Her.
Earning her living. On her feet, sometimes. On her
back—

JACQUELINE: Don't—

EUGENE: He should know! Everything you had to do!
To put food into our stomachs! Till Harry Seitz came
along. Thinking he could somehow rescue us. Pull us
right out of our misery. With his money. And power.
And position. And when he left us, like I always knew
he would, I used what I'd learned about him and his
financial dealings to get me the same things.

NICHOLAS: You blackmailed him.

EUGENE: Hey, that son of a bitch has been trading on
inside information since day one.

NICHOLAS: And then you went about your stated business.

EUGENE: You got it.

NICHOLAS: To bring about the destruction of my family.

EUGENE: Dead on.

NICHOLAS: Me.

EUGENE: Well, obviously.

NICHOLAS: Rachel.

EUGENE: Sure.

NICHOLAS: Rachel's brother. Her mother. Her father.

EUGENE: Everybody.

NICHOLAS: My mother.

EUGENE: Like I said.

NICHOLAS: And my father.

EUGENE: He was the first. I set him up and knocked him down. And he walked right into that plane. Right into that propeller. Man, what a mess. *(Pause)* So how about it? Revenge? Is that still on the menu?

NICHOLAS: Yes. Oh, yes.

EUGENE: What are you waiting for?

(NICHOLAS *looks at* EUGENE. *He looks at the gun in his hand. He raises it up and points it at* EUGENE's *head.* NICHOLAS's *body is shaking. A moment)*

JACQUELINE: Please, don't.

EUGENE: He won't. He *can't.*

NICHOLAS: I *could.* Even here. In front of her. I could pull back on this trigger and blow you away. You'd be gone.

EUGENE: Well?

(Nothing. NICHOLAS *slowly lowers the gun to his side. He carefully puts it back in the box. He returns it to* EUGENE. EUGENE *smiles.)*

EUGENE: See, Mom? What did I tell you? The man knows I'm right.

NICHOLAS: What I *know* is that what happened to you and your mother was wrong. It was worse than wrong. It was wicked. Sinful. Evil. And, yes, in some way, I might actually have been responsible. But I know something else.

EUGENE: What's that?

*(*NICHOLAS *only stares at* EUGENE.*)*

EUGENE: You think you deserve to live.

NICHOLAS: I'm going to walk out of this building, Eugene. I'm going to gather up my life. And I'm going to find a way, I swear I am—

(Pause)

EUGENE: To what?

*(*NICHOLAS *shakes his head.)*

EUGENE: What?

NICHOLAS: You wouldn't understand.

EUGENE: Try me.

*(*NICHOLAS *starts to go.)*

EUGENE: I can't let you walk out that door, coz. *(He pulls the gun out of the box, places the box on a table, and aims the weapon at* NICHOLAS.*)* It wouldn't be right.

JACQUELINE: Eugene, you said—

EUGENE: Not to the memory of my family.

NICHOLAS: Please—

JACQUELINE: You said that we'd never actually hurt anyone!

EUGENE: I said that?

JACQUELINE: That we'd only take things away! The way they were taken away from us!

EUGENE: I was lying.

JACQUELINE: Eugene!

(JACQUELINE *reaches for the gun and the action seems to shift into slow motion. The lighting changes. A thundering heartbeat is heard.* EUGENE *pushes his mother away. She grabs hold of him and attempts to wrestle the weapon from his grasp. They fall to the floor. The guns goes off. The room goes red.*)

EUGENE: Mom...?

JACQUELINE: Oh, my God.

EUGENE: Mother?

JACQUELINE: Oh, sweet Jesus.

EUGENE: I...I didn't—

JACQUELINE: I'm bleeding.

EUGENE: MOM!

NICHOLAS: I'll get help.

(AMELIA *enters as* NICHOLAS *starts to exit. He passes her. He stops. Then he turns and looks at her. She turns and looks at him. For a moment their eyes lock. Dead silence*)

AMELIA: Don't forget.

NICHOLAS: What?

AMELIA: Forgiveness.

NICHOLAS: Grandma?

AMELIA: Forgiveness.

NICHOLAS: It *is* you.

AMELIA: My Nicky.

(AMELIA *comes to* NICHOLAS. *She runs her hands through his hair. He shakes his head.*)

NICHOLAS: What happened to us?

(AMELIA *turns away from him and slowly moves through the room. She sings.* NICHOLAS *backs out of the room.*)

AMELIA: In the winter night when our skin is white,
We will cease our endless strife,

(JACQUELINE *rises and slowly leaves the stage.*)

AMELIA: And the plans we made will finally fade
As we let go of this life.

(EUGENE *stands and slowly leaves the stage.*)

AMELIA: And our children's children now may know
The sorrow of our days...

Scene 10

(RACHEL *enters as* AMELIA *exits. She carries the journal with her. She sits at the table with a lit cigarette in her hand. She reads aloud. We are once again in the attic of the family house in Evansville.*)

RACHEL: Maybe I made a mistake in leaving Eugene alone holding the body of his mother because when I got back with the police, the paramedics—

(*The sound of another gunshot.*)

RACHEL: He was dead. (*Pause*) I stayed up all that night and most of the next day attempting to explain my story to the authorities. Nothing I said made much sense. Finally they let me go. But not before I found myself in the very strange position of identifying the body of Eugene Barnes and his mother, Jacqueline. After all, I was the next of kin. (*Pause*) I considered my options. Harrison Seitz had evidently dropped all charges again me, but I could continue in my efforts to persecute *him.* I could tell my story to the press. The world. Anyone who would listen. I considered carefully. I walked to the bus station, begged for money, and traveled east.

(NICHOLAS *enters. He is putting on a clean shirt. He watches* RACHEL *read.)*

RACHEL: When I first began this journal I had no idea why I was doing it. Or who I was writing it for. Now I know. *(Pause)* It was for you, Rachel. I kept this diary for you. *(She closes the book. She turns and looks at him.)* You're clean.

NICHOLAS: Yeah.

RACHEL: Found some clothes?

NICHOLAS: They might have been my dad's. Or his dad's.

RACHEL: So what will you do?

NICHOLAS: Stay here. For a few days. Maybe longer. *(Pause)* If that's alright with you.

RACHEL: Sure. Like I said. It's your house, too. *(She touches the journal.)* I can't even talk about this right now.

NICHOLAS: Me, neither.

RACHEL: I'm just glad that you're okay.

(NICHOLAS *takes this in and nods. Then he goes to the window and opens it. There is stillness now after the storm.)*

NICHOLAS: It looks like somebody's been chopping down those weeds.

RACHEL: That would be me.

NICHOLAS: Oh?

RACHEL: The soil's good. I checked. We could grow almost anything out there.

NICHOLAS: We?

RACHEL: Mm-hmm.

NICHOLAS: I don't know the first thing about farming.

RACHEL: Oh, like I do?

(Pause)

NICHOLAS: What I'm saying is it's ridiculous.

RACHEL: Uh-huh.

NICHOLAS: Absurd.

RACHEL: Okay. *(Pause)* I'll do it myself.

(RACHEL puts the journal down on the table and starts to go. NICHOLAS shakes his head. He looks back out the window.)

NICHOLAS: I mean, what would we grow?

(We hear the distant sound of AMELIA singing.)

AMELIA: We will then restore to the land once more, To the marigolds and maize.

(NICHOLAS continues to stare out into the night. RACHEL stands in the doorway looking at him.)

END OF PLAY

Amelia's Song

Moderate ♩ = 90

Music and Lyrics by Douglas Post

In the sum-mer light when the fields are bright with the mar-i-golds and maize, we will run with o-pen arms out-stretched to the start-ing___ of our days. We will run so fast, we will run so far, we will set out to___ be-gin, but the sum-mer heat and fields of wheat will nev-er___ come a-gain. In the win-ter night when the earth is white, we will lay our bod-ies down and those things we feel and hold as real will drift a-way and drown. Through the dark-ened world, we will fall un-furled to the fin-ish of___ our days, In the reel-ing black, we'll then reach back to the mar-i-golds and maize, to the mar-i-golds___ and maize. In the sum-mer light when the

© 2017 by Douglas Post

fields are bright and the sky is full of praise, we will fill our cup and lift it up to the

starting of our days, we will make our schemes, we will dream our dreams with no

why or where or when, but that fra-grant wine that was so fine will nev - er come a-

gain. In the win - ter night when our skin is white, we will cease our end -

less strife, and the plans we made will fi - n'lly fade as we let go of this life. And our

chil-dren's chil-dren now may know the sor-row of ___ our days. We will then re-store

to the land once more, ___ to the mar - i - golds and maize.